"People say three-star cooking is safe, but it isn't.
It's the most dangerous thing I know."

GORDON RAMSAY

★ ★ ★

CHEF

PHOTOGRAPHS BY *Quentin Bacon*

KEY PORTER  BOOKS

CONTENTS

I'm often asked where my passion for cooking comes from. Where did the great adventure all begin, and what's propelled me to the position I'm in now? To tell the truth, I've often wondered the same thing myself. All I know is that the moment I walked into a professional kitchen as a pimply 17-year-old, proudly clutching my first set of knives, I knew I'd found my purpose in life. From that day on, my sole ambition was to win three stars, and nothing was going to stand in my way.

Some people argue that it was the lean times of my childhood, growing up in subsidized housing and surviving on powdered milk because there was nothing to pay the milkman, that ignited my lifelong obsession with food. I'll leave that to the amateur psychologists, but it was a few years later, in France, that I realised just how deep that passion was and everything really clicked into place. I had been working at Le Gavroche in London, and Albert Roux had obviously seen something in me, so he sent me to work for Guy Savoy and then Joël Robuchon in Paris. For the first time I felt completely free. No interruptions, no emotional baggage from my parents, no obstruction from previous mentors. I was completely cut off. I wouldn't even contact home for fear of breaking my focus.

I'd work double, even triple shifts in the kitchens, and then as a waiter in my time off. I was desperate to learn everything I could about the French respect for ingredients, their desire to get everything absolutely right. I almost became more French than the French themselves.

I guess that's where the passion is—in making every element of a meal as perfect as it possibly can be. To misquote Bill Shankly, cooking isn't a matter of life and death, it's more important than that. That's why once or twice a year I wake up in a cold sweat, panicking about losing my third star. But if it happens, I'll just work my bollocks off and win it back again.

What do they mean, those elusive stars that have come to symbolize the hopes and dreams of every aspiring chef; those badges of honour—years in the winning, moments in the losing—that dominate kitchen life from first thing in the morning until last thing at night? And what does it take to join the elite three-star chefs in the world's most exclusive club? Michelin issues no guidelines. There is no formula, no crib to tell restaurateurs what the team of anonymous inspectors is looking for.

The only intimation is that stars are awarded simply for what is on the plate. Inspectors are assessing the quality of ingredients, the skill in preparing them, the flair for combining flavours, the level of creativity and, above all, consistency.

In practice, a single star rewards above-average cooking for the class of restaurant it is in, be it a relaxed restaurant or formal hotel dining room. A second star reflects greater refinement across the whole meal, more imagination in the kitchen, and the use of higher quality ingredients, of *produit noble* as the French call it.

A third star is rarely awarded. Here, Michelin is looking for something truly exceptional, a complete mastery of the whole gastronomic process—from leading and inspiring a team to delivering faultless cooking at every service, every day, every week. There is no room for error: the *amuse-bouche* that opens the meal must be as perfect as the *petits fours* that close it.

Few two-star chefs have it in them to make that final leap. To succeed, they must show remarkable originality, invention, and the ability to adapt. They must also inject their own personality into their cuisine, and let their character come through. A three-star chef must provide the magic, passion, and excitement that enables the diner to sense that anything is possible—something that Gordon Ramsay has always understood.

"In a three-star restaurant we expect cooking of the highest quality—for it to show flair, finesse, and balance. But more than that, we expect the cook's personality to show through. And that's what Gordon Ramsay has always done. He is a supremely talented chef, able to inspire his team to produce exceptional cooking on a regular basis."

DEREK BROWN, DIRECTOR OF THE MICHELIN GUIDE, 2000–4

"Sensitivity, passion, strength—these are the words to define Gordon Ramsay, a man who has helped bring cooking to a point we could only dream of a few years ago. After reading this book, we will understand why eating well nourishes the soul."

FERRAN ADRIÀ, EL BULLI

"Running a restaurant is like putting on a live show every day—but without a script."

The cast assembles at 7am every morning, five days a week, backstage in the kitchen of Royal Hospital Road. Silently and in total concentration, they rehearse their roles: preparing up to 15 sauces from stocks that have been bubbling away overnight; prepping the vegetables; filleting the fish;

par-cooking the risotto; or caramelizing the tarte tatins to be finished off during service. This five-hour *mise-en-place* ahead of lunch is when the majority of the work is done. Front of house Jean-Claude, Gordon's long-serving *maître d'*, casts a final eye over the dining room to make sure that every

glass, every piece of tableware is in place. Soon the audience will take their seats and expect another flawless performance. Better than anyone, Gordon knows that running a restaurant is like putting on a show, a self-contained drama in three acts. People come to be fed, but they also come to be entertained.

The smile on arrival, the discreet service, the playfulness of a pineapple and chili soup —all are calculated to bring that buzz of excitement. "It has to be dramatic because customers vote with their feet. If they aren't excited by the way they eat, they won't come back. It's as simple as that."

AND SO THE SHOW BEGINS. As in any three-star restaurant, this is signalled by the arrival of the *amuse-bouches*, literally "entertainments for the mouth." Their gastronomic function is to get the tastebuds going, to tease the palate with the promise of the delights to follow. More than this, though, they help to put diners at their ease as they settle into their new surroundings, drawing their focus to the task in hand—to surrender to the unalloyed luxury that is a three-star meal.

PAN-FRIED SCALLOPS WITH A MILLEFEUILLE OF POTATO,
PARMESAN VELOUTÉ, AND TRUFFLE BUTTONS

NOW THE KITCHEN MOVES INTO GEAR. A pre-appetizer is dispatched, again to heighten anticipation but also to win the chefs a little more time to prepare the first dish to be cooked to order. "You don't want to give guests time to get bored, or they'll start picking holes in the décor. Their appetizers should be on the table within 15 minutes of ordering, max."

"We create new dishes by constantly evolving the old ones. Ideas can come at any time, but often it is during service when you're busy and all the creative juices are flowing. You'll be dressing a plate at the pass and think… What if I tweaked the sauce, or added such and such from this dish to that one? Four or five menus down the line, a dish could have changed so much you wouldn't recognize it from the original dish that was its inspiration.

"That said, there are some dishes we will never change. My ravioli of lobster, langoustine, and salmon, served here with a lemongrass and chervil velouté, has become a classic. I don't see how it can be improved in any way. It shows great technique and skill, and customers have complained when we've tried to take it off the menu."

RAVIOLI OF LOBSTER, LANGOUSTINE, AND SALMON WITH
A LEMONGRASS AND CHERVIL VELOUTÉ

"We serve lobster in all sorts of different ways, including at one time with a carpaccio of scallops. One day the weather was too bad in Scotland for the boats to go out, so we tried using some very thinly sliced octopus instead. It worked even better than the scallops and an instant classic was born. Sometimes it happens like that—your arm is forced and you end up improving a dish out of adversity."

SALAD OF LOBSTER WITH OCTOPUS CARPACCIO,
ROASTED WATERMELON, BABY SQUID,
AND A SHELLFISH SAUCE

"The minute you send a dish you're not
100 percent happy with, you might as well go home.
Game over."

Gordon, his head chef Simone, and sous-chef Clare are gathered around the pass, tasting a salad of lobster, roasted watermelon, and baby squid. Gordon isn't happy. "These calamari, they've been fried 10 seconds too long," he says. The rings of battered squid look a perfect golden brown, but in Gordon's eyes they are an abomination. "How do I know that? Because they should melt in your mouth, but we're all still chewing on the bloody things now. They've got to be in, out, seasoned, and gone."

Gordon says he's never sent a dish he wasn't entirely happy with, thinking, never mind, we'll get it right next time. "If it wasn't perfect, it should never have left the kitchen."

SEARED LOIN OF TUNA WITH
POACHED VEAL FILET, SPRING TRUFFLES,
AND CAPER DRESSING

CARPACCIO OF TUNA AND SWORDFISH WITH A
MIXED HERB SALAD AND BROWN BUTTER DRESSING

"We have used a lot of red mullet over the years. Originally, we served the fish with a light soup made from the bones, then we started using the same stock to make a beautiful creamy risotto. From there we changed the rice to pearl barley, and that's how this dish was born."

FILLET OF RED MULLET
WITH COD, GREEN ONION, AND PEARL BARLEY RISOTTO,
AND A SWEET AND SOUR PEPPER SAUCE

"The first question, always, is are we delivering on flavour?"

A chef's palate is his greatest asset. The art of tasting is the first lesson everyone in Gordon's kitchens must learn. Make the sauce, taste it, season it, taste it, finish it, taste it. Every morning, his head chefs will be brought a succession of dishes to test: the day's foams, mousses, and creams from the pastry section; vinaigrettes and ballotines of foie gras from cold appetizers; and so on. Every one must be tasted and compared against a sensory memory bank of flavours.

But how do you sharpen a chef's palate? Can it be taught at all? Gordon regularly holds blindfolded tasting sessions, when the chefs try each other's dishes and attempt to identify the ingredients. But, as he admits, you can only take it so far.

"You can teach taste up to a certain level, but you can't perfect it. You can open the door, but you can't lead them through it. I can't impose my palate on others, but what I try to do is to teach my chefs confidence, to rely on their own senses. It's not a snob thing, it's not about being sophisticated —I've proved that, coming from my humble background. It's about identifying the key element of each and every dish and focusing in on it, to the exclusion of everything else."

BALLOTINE OF FOIS GRAS WITH LABEL ANGLAIS
CHICKEN, MARINATED SHIMEJI MUSHROOMS, AND
A PORT VINAIGRETTE

PRESSED FOIE GRAS WITH SAUTERNES
AND CHAMOMILE JELLY, SERVED WITH TRUFFLE BRIOCHE

FRICASSÉE OF SNAILS WITH SPINACH, BABY ARTICHOKES,
MUSHROOMS, PANCETTA, AND JERUSALEM ARTICHOKE PURÉE

"The snails we use are beautifully plump and sweet and come from a farm in Dorset. I love that. This seems such a classically French dish and of course, in essence, it is, but we've brought it wholesale across the Channel."

"This was an interesting one. We did a classic steak tartare with a soft poached quail egg on top; a scallop tartare topped with a deep layer of caviar was also on the menu. At the time we were using Japanese Kobe beef, which is very rich, and I wondered what it would be like to have a spoonful of salty caviar with it, to cut the richness a bit. This strange-sounding combination worked even better than I had imagined. I have since learned that the Japanese have been doing it for years, so great minds clearly think alike."

TARTARE OF BEEF FILET WITH OSCIETRA CAVIAR
AND MARINATED RED AND YELLOW PEPPERS

"Nothing beats the excitement when the first winter truffles come in—first the black ones from Perigord and then white truffles from Alba. We use summer truffles mainly for decoration."

PAN-GRILLED ASPARAGUS WITH SEL DE GUÉRANDE,
SERVED WITH A TOMATO VINAIGRETTE

SALAD OF ASPARAGUS, BABY ARTICHOKES, AND PERIGORD TRUFFLES
WITH A CREAMY TRUFFLE DRESSING

"Every meal should be in harmony.

You must find that perfect balance."

A good meal is like a well-orchestrated piece of chamber music. It should consist of swells and lulls, of melodies and counterpoints. Just as the conductor draws the listener from the opening prelude to the grand finale, so the chef leads the diner irresistibly from appetizer to dessert. There is no point crushing the palate with a powerful appetizer only to follow it with a delicate fish course. It would be lost. Equally, the components of every dish must not compete with each other.

"I always think in terms of textures and flavours. I'd never team a harsh herb like rosemary with something delicate like scallops. It would be too powerful—better a soft herb such as chervil or tarragon. The downfall of many chefs is that they pick at their food but never eat it as a customer would. So they forget that they have to maintain that magic—not just on the first mouthful, but across the whole dish. That's the hard bit, getting that balance on a plate."

BUTTERNUT SQUASH VELOUTÉ WITH SAUTÉED CÈPES, PARMESAN CRISP, AND
MUSHROOM AND WHITE TRUFFLE TORTELLINI

As the components of a dish become ready, chefs will carry them to the pass, where the head chef assembles them on the plate and adds the finishing touches, perhaps a micro salad of slender pea shoots and leaves, or a dramatic parmesan crisp. Then a final inspection before it is whisked through to the dining room. "We never add anything just for the sake of ornament. Every garnish has to earn its place as an integral part of the dish."

CHILLED TOMATO CONSOMMÉ WITH ASPARAGUS, PEAS,
TOMATO CONCASSÉ, AND BASIL

Not so long ago, the sommelier struck a terrifying figure as he stalked the dining room, silver tastevin dangling self-importantly from his neck. He (and it always was a he) would sneer at our ignorance and humiliate us into delving more expensively into the list. The modern sommelier, by contrast, as often a woman as a man, is far more approachable and less chauvinistic in his loyalty to France. The list at Royal Hospital Road, rightly acknowledged to be one of the most impressive in the world, draws its bins from all the regions of the world, from North America to New Zealand, and, yes, taking in a bit of France on the way. And the sommeliers are as happy to recommend a bottle for £30 as for £3,000.

"Restaurants shouldn't be stiff and formal. They should be fun—and part of that fun is in trying things you haven't had before. I always ask a sommelier for a recommendation when I go out. After all, they should know the list better than anyone else, and know the dishes they are matching the wine to."

Main courses are the more straightforward dishes in Gordon Ramsay's repertoire, where the principal ingredient is allowed to sing. It's not just to keep the number of flavours to a minimum, but for a very practical reason. A fillet of salmon will carry on cooking on the plate, a sliced loin of pork will grow cold and dry out, so that means working fast. You don't want to be messing around with fancy presentation. In fact, the simpler the better. "On to the plate, out to the dining room, job done."

LINE-CAUGHT TURBOT ROASTED ON THE BONE,
WITH A GARNISH OF STUFFED BABY PEPPERS AND SPRING VEGETABLES

PAN-ROASTED FILLET OF JOHN DORY
WITH CRAB, CRUSHED NEW POTATOES,
AND A BASIL VINAIGRETTE

"I first served John Dory on a bed of crushed new potatoes flavoured with olives and tomatoes, and a chopped tomato vinaigrette. This dish is pretty much still the same, but with the addition of fresh crab to the potatoes and a fine basil purée to the dressing."

PAN-GRILLED MONKFISH WITH CONFIT DUCK,

RED AND YELLOW PEPPERS,

AND A RED WINE SAUCE

"If you can't get the small things right,
what hope is there for the big stuff, like the cooking?"

Every morning, while those around them are preparing for the day's two services, the head chefs at Royal Hospital Road are brought a glass of freshly squeezed orange juice and a slice from every loaf of bread. It's not a late breakfast—just the first in a long line of tastings to make sure everything is as it should be. It isn't unusual to taste different oranges from several countries, or a blend of them, before the juice passes muster.

Gordon's empire may stretch over fourteen restaurants and four continents, he may have ten Michelin stars to his name, but like all successful people he has never lost sight of the small things on which his success is built. Be it the positioning of a wine glass, the seasoning of the bread, the colour of a Bloody Mary—he knows that it is by such details that he will be judged. "You have to get those right. They set the tone for the rest of the evening."

"This halibut dish started life with a pink grapefruit vinaigrette, the tartness of which offset the sweetness of the fish. The grapefruit changed to orange and then to passion fruit, which we are still using, as its perfumed tartness is perfect with halibut."

HALIBUT FILLETS LARDED WITH SMOKED SALMON,
SERVED WITH CANDIED LEMON, BRAISED VEGETABLES,
AND SMOKED HORSERADISH VELOUTÉ

PAN-FRIED SEA BASS WITH ROASTED BABY ARTICHOKES,
BORLOTTI BEANS, AND A CÈPE VELOUTÉ

"Cooking fish is one of the biggest tests of any chef. It needs a deft touch and is much less forgiving than a piece of meat. Timing is all. To serve a stunning fillet of sea bass or line-caught turbot roasted on the bone is an act of such simplicity, yet it requires total confidence in your technique and in your raw ingredients. There's nowhere to hide with fish."

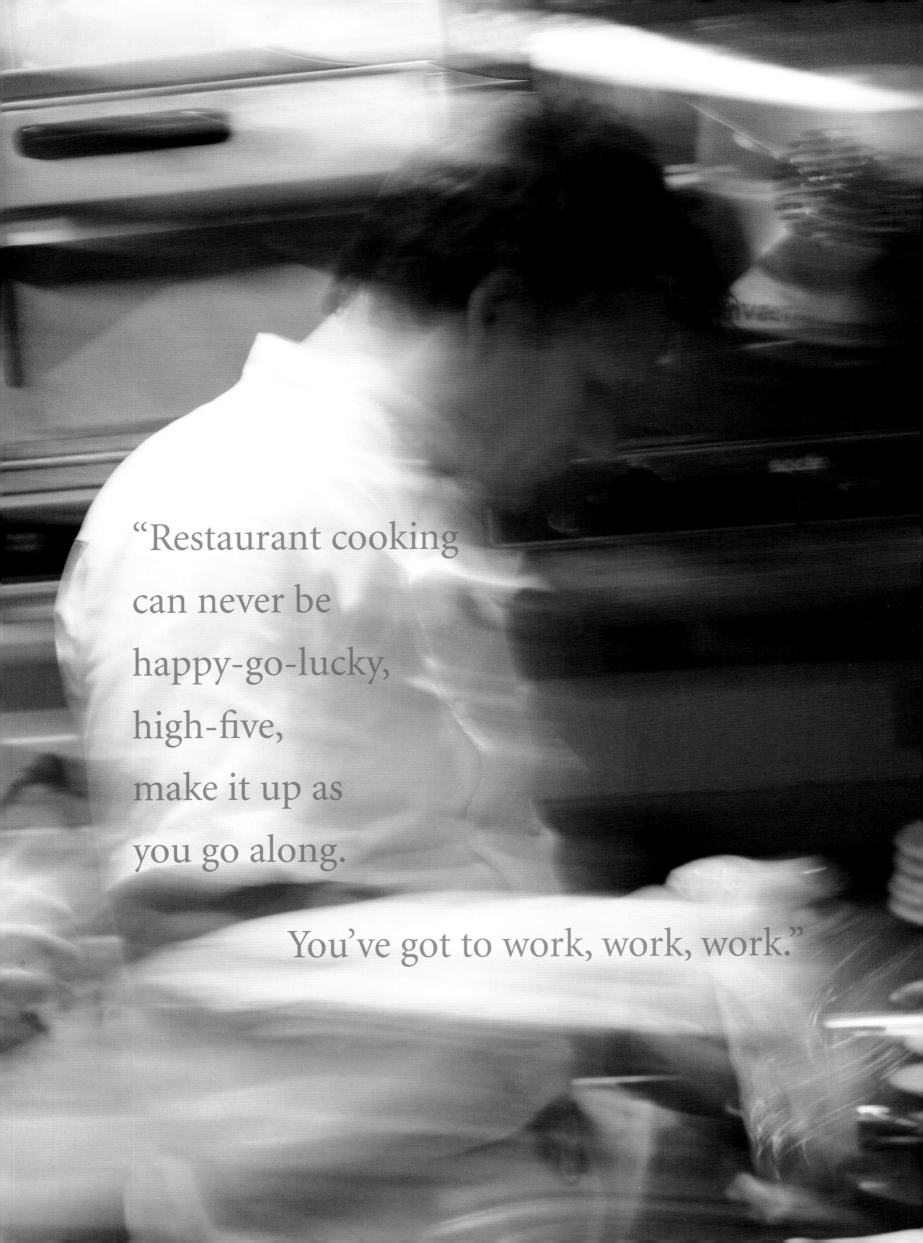

"Restaurant cooking
can never be
happy-go-lucky,
high-five,
make it up as
you go along.

You've got to work, work, work."

There's a common misconception that cooking is an art: all visionary genius and leaps of creative faith. In the best chefs, that certainly plays a part—the ability to conjure up an epoch-defining dish must come from within—but at its heart, cooking is a craft, one learned through repetition and adherence to an established set of culinary principles. It's only once these have been fully understood and mastered that a chef can move on to a higher plane. In other words, there's no substitute for graft.

And no one can complain that Gordon hasn't put in the hard work. He has paid his dues under some of the most talented chefs in Europe, from Marco Pierre White and Michel Roux to Guy Savoy and Joël Robuchon, often taking a cut in pay and status in order to complete his training. When he left Le Gavroche in London for Restaurant Guy Savoy in Paris, for example, he went from head chef to kitchen porter effectively, only to work his way up again.

His reward now is that there's not a job he will ask one of his chefs to do that he cannot do better, be it boning a pig's foot, filleting a turbot, or making a classic beurre blanc. "I was determined never to be fazed or intimidated by an ingredient, to stand in front of it and not know exactly what to do with it. At Guy Savoy I used to watch the others peel cèpes and then dry out the peelings to make cèpe powder, which would crop up in a risotto three weeks later. They never told me what they were doing, I had to work it out myself."

"When making a capon bouillon, they'd start by filtering the water through cheesecloth, and the second it started simmering, they would ladle off the scum every 2 minutes for hours on end. I didn't understand why at first, but 8 hours later they ended up with a stock so crystal clear there was no need to clarify it. You can't help but see something like that and pick up on the brilliance of it."

ROASTED BRESSE SQUAB WRAPPED IN PROSCIUTTO WITH FOIE GRAS, CREAMED MUSHROOMS, AND A DATE SAUCE

ROASTED DUCK BREAST WITH HONEY-GLAZED BABY ONIONS
AND SALSIFY, MINTED PEAS, AND A MADEIRA SAUCE

"You don't get to run a three-star kitchen by sitting

If Harvey's, where Gordon Ramsay trained under Marco Pierre White for two years, was known as the S.A.S. of kitchens, a spell in his own has been compared to a tour of duty in Vietnam. The days are long—starting at 7am and often not finishing until 1am—and the casualty rate is high. One in two new recruits doesn't last the month.

"It's a hard environment, I don't make any excuse for that. It's hot, it's high pressure, and you've got to be physically and mentally fit. But that's kitchens for you: there's no room for fat chefs any more, and if you don't put in the hours, you'll never learn."

on your backside 16 hours a day."

ROASTED LOIN OF VENISON WITH BRAISED RED CABBAGE AND PARSNIP CHIPS

NAVARIN OF LAMB WITH BUTTERED VEGETABLES,
CELERIAC PURÉE, AND THYME JUS

"This dish—featuring two cuts of lamb—is always on my menu, even if the garnish changes regularly. The combination of the 'posh cut' of rack and the 'cheap cut' of shoulder is fantastic. We cook the shoulder very slowly for several hours, then pick the meat off the bone and remove any sinew. Then we press it, cut out rounds, and pan-fry them until crisp on the outside and soft in the middle. It may be the cheaper cut, but the result is phenomenal."

RACK OF LAMB WITH CONFIT SHOULDER, PROVENÇALE VEGETABLES, SPINACH, AND BASIL LAMB JUS

is a fight you have to win. You're up against yourself every time."

A box of artichokes has arrived at Royal Hospital Road for that day's lunch special: a salad of baby artichokes with asparagus and fresh truffles. A commis is peeling them by hand. In a lazy kitchen, they'd be dowsed in white wine vinegar to stop them going brown, but no such shortcuts here. Instead the commis' fingers work faster and faster, racing against time before the artichokes start to oxidize. That's the level of self-discipline needed in a three-star kitchen, where every ingredient must be treated the best way possible.

"At Guy Savoy, I learned to handle every ingredient like a piece of precious jewelry. He would have me blowing the grit out of hundreds of morels with a hairdryer like I was Vidal Sassoon, but to see them later, served up sautéed on top of a white truffle risotto, was mind-blowing. Each one of them blow-dried to perfection—all that work for a single moment of pleasure. That's how I learned to respect every single ingredient, to see it for all its potential and make it as perfect as it can be."

ROASTED FILET OF BEEF WITH A TRUFFLE AND
ROOT VEGETABLE INFUSION

"The more confident a chef,
the less he needs to hide."

Ask Gordon his favourite dish and the answer is the same every time. Not the tagliatelle of oysters and caviar he learned at Harvey's; not his own slow-braised pork belly with creamed celeriac and Madeira sauce; but something he ate nearly 20 years ago in a simple restaurant in the Pyrenees—breast of lamb with roasted apricots and boulangère potatoes. "And that was it, just three things on the plate. It wasn't pretty, there were no frills, but with all the will in the world, no one could have made it better."

It typifies what he tries to achieve in his own cooking. Yes, there's lobster, caviar, foie gras, and truffles aplenty at Royal Hospital Road, but you'll find no symphonies of this nestling in beds of that, just four or five clean flavours on a plate. "I'm always pulling back from adding more elements to a dish, always asking, 'Can I make this simpler?' Young chefs who lack confidence use frills and decoration as a security blanket, to mask the lack of focus on flavour. They think that if it looks good, it will taste good. But that's the wrong message. I always tell them to take a third off the plate and start again." It's a mistake he made himself in the early days of Aubergine, "because of the insecurity you feel when you're starting out." There were some dishes that were so over-complicated that only he could finish them off. He'd have his brigade prep the carrots this way, the leeks that way, and at midday they still had no idea how the dishes would be put together. "Sure, it was exciting, but that's no way to run a kitchen. You couldn't do that in a three-star kitchen."

"Slow-braised pork belly is a cut that will never leave my menus. It's so versatile that I've changed this dish around too many ways to number. We've served it with squid, with lobster, with langoustines, even with deep-fried quail eggs. It's one of my favourites and has been with me since the very beginning."

SLOW-BRAISED PORK BELLY WITH LANGOUSTINE,
CRUSHED PEAS, AND MADEIRA SAUCE,
SERVED WITH CRISPY LACED PORK RIND (ABOVE)

PORK CHEEKS WITH PORK FILET WRAPPED IN PROSCIUTTO,
BLACK PUDDING, BABY TURNIPS, AND SAUTÉED MORELS

VEAL OSSO BUCCO WITH BOULANGÈRE POTATOES, SAVOY CABBAGE,
TURNIP PURÉE, AND ITS OWN BRAISING JUS

Risotto of Cèpes

with green onions, grated truffle, and parmesan

"Our risottos and the way we flavour and finish them has changed dramatically over the years. Fresh cèpes are a dream to use, but very expensive. A sprinkling of cèpe powder—made by drying out the peelings in a low oven and pulverizing them—is a great way to finish a cèpe risotto. We used to enrich this risotto with whipped cream but it made the whole thing too creamy, so now we just use butter, a little mascarpone, and parmesan. It's the way the Italians do it, and you can't argue with that."

"There are people who think that Gordon has been lucky, but I'm not one of them. Determination, skill, bloody-mindedness, and hard work—these are the reasons for his success... This is his luck."

ALBERT ROUX

THE ONLY EXCEPTION TO THE MANTRA OF SIMPLIFICATION IS WITH DESSERTS. "That's the grand finale, that's the payoff, where you can stare at a perfect caramelized pear tatin or a beautifully presented bitter chocolate mousse with coffee granita for several minutes and think... wow!"

CARAMELIZED PEAR TATIN WITH GORGONZOLA ICE CREAM AND WALNUT CREAM

"How can you improve on perfection?

Well, I'll have a bloody good try."

CARAMELIZED APPLE TARTE TATIN WITH VANILLA ICE CREAM

"The tarte tatin is a classic. Whether we do it with apples or pears, plums or clementines, the principles are the same. Where we try to improve on this near perfect dish is by flavouring the caramel—with rosemary, cinnamon, or star anise, for example. Cardamom is a brilliant spicy addition and walnuts give a great taste, too."

CARROT AND WHITE CHOCOLATE FONDANT WITH DARK CHOCOLATE SORBET

TOFFEE SOUFFLÉ WITH BANANA AND LIME ICE CREAM

LEMON MERINGUE WITH MARINATED STRAWBERRIES

PLUM CRUMBLE TART WITH ALMOND FRANGIPANE

A menu can never stand still. Diners want to be enticed into trying new things, to share the excitement coming from the kitchen, so a chef must reinvent or die. But at this level, innovation brings its own risks and the stakes are high. At any time, three-quarters of the menu at Royal Hospital Road comprises tried and tested "classics"; the rest are new dishes, which may in turn become regular fixtures.

RASPBERRY COMPOTE WITH TARRAGON CREAM

MARINATED PINEAPPLE RAVIOLI WITH MANGO, BERRIES,
AND MINT SORBET

PINEAPPLE AND CHILI SOUP
WITH FROMAGE BLANC FOAM

In the old days, cooks were far more restricted in the roles they took. They trained as sauce chefs, pastry chefs, fish and meat chefs—and there they stayed. Gordon has always been determined that his kitchen would be different, that his chefs should have an understanding of all the different sections. One result is a greater cross-fertilization of ideas. The pastry (or dessert) section is a good example. "Ten years ago, who would have thought we would now be adding salt to a caramel; basil or bay leaves to a crème anglaise; or chili to ice cream?" He has taken desserts onto a whole new level.

SABLÉ BRETON WITH RASPBERRIES, VANILLA CREAM,
AND VANILLA ICE CREAM

TIRAMISU WITH COFFEE GRANITA

APPLE PARFAIT WITH HONEYCOMB, BITTER CHOCOLATE, AND CHAMPAGNE FOAM

"Pastry has always been the most creative section, the one where chefs can let their imaginations really run wild."

Often separated from the hubbub of the main kitchen, the pastry chefs can patiently tease out their creations in relative solitude. The mornings are spent preparing their mousses and creams, their granitas and ice creams, their tuiles and cakes, leaving them a luxury during service denied to their colleagues—that of time. You can't hurry artistry like this.

PALET D'OR WITH CHOCOLATE AND HAZELNUT ICE CREAM
AND PASSION FRUIT CREAM

SLOW-BAKED QUINCE WITH CRÈME CATALAN, PEDRO XIMENEZ GELÉE,
AND ACACIA HONEY GRANITA

"A classic of mine since my Aubergine days, this is basically

a small taster of the desserts on the menu and is served for two.

The li... ...changes regularly, but we often fini...... ....miniature soufflés."

"Cubes, waves, pyramids, cylinders—
chocolate is the perfect foil for the
pastry chef's dark art."

CHOCOLATE PARFAIT WITH PASSION FRUIT
AND GUAVA COULIS

BITTER CHOCOLATE MOUSSE WITH COFFEE GRANITA AND LIGHT GINGER CREAM

"Cheese is another area where we used to bow to the French, but British cheeses are so good now they make up nearly half our board."

THE ARRIVAL OF THE PETITS FOURS SIGNALS THE END OF THE 3-STAR EXPERIENCE. The curtain is about to go down on another bravura performance. This is the final chance to linger, to have one last taste as a reminder of the brilliance that has preceded it. And then it's all over, the last mouthful as extravagantly exquisite as the first.

"Whatever
happens during
a tough service,
every mistake stays
in the kitchen."

12.30am. Another day comes to an end. As the last customers make their way home, there are supplies to be ordered; fridges to be cleaned; floors to scrub; stoves to be polished "until you can see your own reflection, because that's the first thing that greets you when you start your day." It's also the time when the kitchen becomes the dressing room, a place for post-game reflection and analysis. Talk turns to what went right, what went wrong, "how when I said four minutes on the hot plate, it was four and a half."

It's also a time for bonding as chefs, waiters, porters—everyone—comes down from the adrenaline rush of a busy service. It's a close-knit team. Because Royal Hospital Road is open only Monday through Friday, the chefs work every shift and many have been with Gordon for more than ten years. They spend more time with each other than they do with their families. Whatever hard words might have been said in the heat of battle, all now is put behind them.

"Then it's lights off, bang. Ready to do it all again the next day."

"Gordon is one of the few chefs in possession of all God's gifts. He's driven, hugely talented at his craft, wickedly funny, a master media-manipulator, able to command and inspire others, and shrewd... very shrewd. One of the few to know what he doesn't know—an unusual saving grace that separates him from other chefs who've tried also to be good businessmen. His dirty little secret is that he's not such a bad bastard after all."

ANTHONY BOURDAIN, BRASSERIE LES HALLES, NEW YORK

THE
RECIPES

APPETIZERS

Pan-fried scallops with a
millefeuille of potato, parmesan
velouté, and truffle buttons

[Recipe on page 134]

Scallops with sweetcorn purée
and quail eggs

[Recipe on page 136]

Mosaic of fruits de mer with
saffron potatoes, tomato
consommé, and oscietra caviar

[Recipe on page 138]

Ravioli of lobster, langoustine, and
salmon with a lemongrass and
chervil velouté

[Recipe on page 140]

Salad of lobster with octopus
carpaccio, roasted watermelon,
baby squid, and a shellfish sauce

[Recipe on page 142]

Seared loin of tuna with poached
veal filet, spring truffles, and
caper dressing

[Recipe on page 144]

Carpaccio of tuna and swordfish
with a mixed herb salad and
brown butter dressing

[Recipe on page 146]

Fillet of red mullet with cod, green
onion, and pearl barley risotto,
and a sweet and sour pepper sauce

[Recipe on page 148]

Ballotine of foie gras with Label
Anglais chicken, marinated shimeji
mushrooms, and a port vinaigrette

[Recipe on page 150]

Pressed foie gras with Sauternes
and chamomile jelly

[Recipe on page 152]

Fricassée of snails with spinach,
baby artichokes, mushrooms,
pancetta, and Jerusalem
artichoke purée

[Recipe on page 154]

Tartare of beef filet with oscietra
caviar and marinated red
and yellow peppers

[Recipe on page 156]

Salad of asparagus, baby artichokes,
and Perigord truffles with a creamy
truffle dressing

[Recipe on page 158]

Pan-grilled asparagus with
sel de Guérande, served with
a tomato vinaigrette

[Recipe on page 160]

Butternut squash velouté with
sautéed cèpes, parmesan crisp, and
mushroom and white truffle
tortellini

[Recipe on page 162]

Chilled tomato consommé with
asparagus, peas, tomato concassé,
and basil

[Recipe on page 164]

Pan-fried scallops with a millefeuille of potato, parmesan velouté, and truffle buttons

THIS IS AN INTERESTING, FUN WAY TO SERVE SCALLOPS, WHICH GO WELL WITH TRUFFLE AND PARMESAN. WE PACK OUR MILLEFEUILLE IN A VACUUM-SEALED BAG TO PRESS THE LAYERS TOGETHER BEFORE POACHING, BUT I HAVE ADJUSTED THE METHOD TO SUIT A DOMESTIC KITCHEN. TO SAVE TIME, YOU COULD FORGO THE TRUFFLE BUTTONS. *[Illustrated on page 18]*

serves 6–8 as an appetizer

MILLEFEUILLE:
½ cup (125 mL) clarified butter (see clarify, page 252)
1¼ lb (625 g) waxy boiling potatoes
Sea salt and black pepper
4 globe artichoke hearts, thinly sliced
3–4 oz (90–100 g) sliced black truffle (or truffle-infused oil for drizzling)

TRUFFLE BUTTONS:
2½ oz (75 g) saffron pasta dough (see page 250)
1 egg white, lightly beaten with 1 tsp (5 mL) water (egg wash)
1 large truffle, thinly sliced

PARMESAN VELOUTÉ:
2 tbsp (30 mL) olive oil
2 large shallots, peeled and finely chopped
Few thyme sprigs
1 bay leaf
1 cup (250 mL) Noilly Prat (or other dry vermouth)
2 cups (500 mL) chicken stock (see page 246)
1 cup (250 mL) whipping cream
1-oz (30-g) piece of parmesan rind (or grated parmesan)

PAN-FRIED SCALLOPS:
9–12 sea scallops, shucked and cleaned
3 tbsp (45 mL) finely grated parmesan
½ tsp (2 mL) mild curry powder
2 tbsp (30 mL) olive oil

FOR GARNISH:
Handful of purple basil (or bull's blood) leaves and baby chard

FIRST, PREPARE THE MILLEFEUILLE. Fill a small roasting pan with 1½ inches (4 cm) of boiling water. Line a 4-cup (1-L) loaf pan with foil, leaving plenty of excess hanging over the sides. Brush the inside of the pan with clarified butter.

PEEL THE POTATOES AND THINLY SLICE using a mandoline. Arrange a layer of potato slices in the bottom of the pan, brush with clarified butter, and season well with salt and pepper. Do the same with the sliced artichokes, then arrange another layer of potato on top, followed by some truffle slices, if using. (Otherwise drizzle with a little truffle oil.) Keep building the layers, brushing lightly with butter and seasoning as you go along. Finish with a top layer of potato, brushed generously with butter.

FOLD THE EXCESS FOIL over to cover the potatoes. Press down firmly and evenly, using a similar-sized pan or the palm of your hand. Carefully lower the loaf pan into the roasting pan. Weight down the millefeuille by placing a similar-sized loaf pan or a small metal tray and a few cans of food on top. Set the roasting pan over low heat and bring to a gentle simmer. Lower the heat until the water is barely simmering and cook until the potatoes throughout are tender when pierced with a metal skewer, 1¼–1½ hours. You may need to replenish the water bath with hot water once or twice during cooking.

REMOVE THE LOAF PAN from the water bath and let the millefeuille cool completely in the pan. Chill for a few hours or overnight until firm, still weighted down.

TO MAKE THE TRUFFLE BUTTONS, roll out the pasta dough as thinly as possible, using a pasta machine. Place the pasta sheet on a lightly floured board and brush with egg wash. Arrange the truffle slices in a single layer on one half of the pasta, then fold over the other half to sandwich the truffle slices. (If you don't have enough truffle to cover half the sheet, just use as much of the pasta as you need.) Using a small cutter (or the top of a large piping tip), stamp out little truffle buttons. Place them on a plate, cover with plastic wrap, and set aside until ready to cook.

FOR THE PARMESAN VELOUTÉ, heat the olive oil in a heavy-based saucepan and sauté the shallots until beginning to soften but not brown, 6–8 minutes. Add the thyme and bay leaf. Deglaze the pan with the vermouth and let bubble until reduced right down. Pour in the stock and boil until reduced by half. Add the cream and parmesan rind. Cook until the sauce has reduced to the consistency of a thick but still pourable cream, 7–10 minutes longer. Strain the velouté through a fine sieve into a clean pan and season with salt and pepper to taste.

JUST BEFORE SERVING, unmould the millefeuille: Peel back the foil and use it to lift the millefeuille, then invert onto a board. Remove the foil and cut the millefeuille into 6–8 thin slices. Heat some of the remaining clarified butter in a large skillet and fry the millefeuille slices until golden brown on both sides, 3–5 minutes. Do this in batches and keep the slices warm in a low oven.

REHEAT THE VELOUTÉ, add the truffle buttons, and cook until the pasta is al dente, about 2 minutes.

CUT EACH SCALLOP horizontally into two discs. Sprinkle one side with the parmesan mixed with the curry powder and a large pinch of salt. Heat the olive oil in a heavy-based skillet until hot, then place the scallops in the pan, coated side down. Cook until golden brown underneath, 1–1½ minutes, then turn. Cook for 1–1½ minutes on the other side; the scallops should feel slightly springy when pressed.

PLACE THREE SCALLOPS, overlapping, in a row on each warm serving plate and lay a slice of millefeuille alongside. Garnish the plates with purple basil and baby chard leaves. Spoon the parmesan velouté over as you serve, making sure that every plate has a few truffle buttons on top of the scallops.

Scallops with sweetcorn purée and quail eggs THIS IS A SIMPLE APPETIZER

THAT CAN BE ASSEMBLED RELATIVELY QUICKLY. THE COMBINATION OF MEATY SCALLOPS, DELICATE

QUAIL EGGS, AND FRAGRANT TRUFFLE IS SUBLIME. *[Illustrated on page 20]*

Serves 6 as an appetizer

SWEETCORN PURÉE:
2 tbsp (30 mL) butter
1 cup (250 mL) frozen corn kernels
1 tsp (5 mL) granulated sugar
¼ cup (50 mL) chicken stock (see page 246)
¼ cup (50 mL) whipping cream
Sea salt and black pepper

TRUFFLE CREAM SAUCE:
¼ cup (50 mL) whipping cream
7 tbsp (105 mL) mayonnaise (see page 249)
1 tsp (5 mL) truffle-infused olive oil
Pinch of minced truffle shavings

SCALLOPS:
9 sea scallops, shucked and cleaned
4 tbsp (60 mL) olive oil
18 quail eggs

FOR SERVING:
1 black truffle (optional)
Lightly dressed salad of mixed leaves (frisée, oak leaf, chervil, etc.)
Olive oil, for drizzling

FIRST, MAKE THE SWEETCORN PURÉE. Melt the butter in a medium pan and add the corn kernels and sugar. Stir over high heat for 1–2 minutes. Add the stock and cream and bring to a boil, then lower the heat and simmer, uncovered, until the corn is soft, about 10 minutes. Transfer the mixture to a food processor and blend for 1–2 minutes until smooth. Push the purée through a fine sieve and discard the pulp. Return the purée to the pan and season with salt and pepper to taste. The sweetcorn purée should be the consistency of thick cream; if it is too thick, add a dash of hot water. Reheat just before serving.

FOR THE TRUFFLE CREAM SAUCE, stir together all the ingredients and season to taste with salt and pepper. Cut half the truffle for serving, if using, into wafer-thin slices and set aside, with the sauce.

CUT EACH SCALLOP horizontally into two discs and season with salt and pepper. Heat a large, heavy-based skillet until very hot, then add half the olive oil. Lay the scallop discs in the pan and cook for 1–1½ minutes on each side; they should feel slightly springy when pressed. Lift them out onto a warm plate and set aside.

NOW COOK THE QUAIL EGGS, in two batches. Heat most of the remaining oil in the pan. Carefully crack the quail eggs open with the tip of a knife and drop them into the hot pan. Fry until the whites are opaque and firm but the yolks are still quite runny, 1–1½ minutes. Remove to a warm plate. Add a little more oil to the pan before you fry the second batch. If you like, use a small pastry cutter to stamp out the fried eggs and neaten the edges.

TO PLATE, arrange three scallop discs on each warm serving plate and top with a wafer-thin slice of truffle and a quail egg. Drop little spoonfuls of warm sweetcorn purée between the scallops. Place a neat handful of mixed salad in the middle, then drizzle the truffle cream sauce and a little olive oil over the top. Finely grate the remaining black truffle, if using, over all. Serve at once.

Mosaic of fruits de mer with saffron potatoes, tomato consommé, and oscietra caviar YOU WILL NEED TO PREPARE THIS SEAFOOD TERRINE A DAY IN ADVANCE, BECAUSE IT NEEDS TO BE PRESSED AND REFRIGERATED OVERNIGHT TO SET. TO SIMPLIFY THE RECIPE, YOU COULD USE ALL HALIBUT OR TURBOT RATHER THAN A COMBINATION, OR SUBSTITUTE ANOTHER FIRM-FLESHED WHITE FISH, SUCH AS MONKFISH. [Illustrated on page 21]

Serves 10–12 as an appetizer

MOSAIC:
12 oz (375 g) salmon fillet, skinned
8 oz (250 g) halibut fillet, skinned
8 oz (250 g) turbot fillet, skinned
12 oz (375 g) centre-cut (thick-cut) tuna fillet
4 cups (1 L) olive oil (approx)
Few thyme sprigs
2 bay leaves
1 tsp (5 mL) rock salt
4 sheets of leaf gelatin ($\frac{1}{2}$ oz/15 g)
1–1$\frac{1}{4}$ cups (250–300 mL) shellfish stock or fish stock (see page 246)
Sea salt and black pepper
2 cooked lobster tails
8 cooked langoustine tails (scampi)
Handful of chives, chervil, tarragon, and dillweed leaves, roughly chopped
Olive oil, for glazing

SAFFRON POTATOES:
2$\frac{1}{2}$ cups (600 mL) vegetable stock (or boiling water)
Large pinch of saffron strands
2 large boiling potatoes
$\frac{1}{4}$ cup (50 mL) classic vinaigrette (see page 249)

FOR SERVING:
1–2 cooked carrots, finely sliced
Few cooked baby onions, sliced and separated into rings
Scant 1 cup (200 mL) chilled tomato consommé (see page 164)
Few chives and chervil, tarragon and dillweed sprigs
10–12 tsp (50–60 mL) oscietra caviar (optional)

TO PREPARE THE MOSAIC, check over the fish fillets for pin bones, removing any you find with tweezers. Pour the olive oil into a deep saucepan and add the thyme, bay leaves, and rock salt. Gently heat the oil until it reaches 130–140°F (55–60°C), checking with a cooking thermometer. You will need to maintain this temperature during cooking by lowering or increasing the heat under the pan.

POACH THE FISH FILLETS in the oil until they feel slightly springy when pressed, indicating they are medium rare: the salmon and tuna should take about 15–20 minutes; the halibut and turbot may be ready in under 15 minutes. (Cook the fish in two batches if your pan is not wide enough.) Carefully lift out the fish with a slotted spoon or spatula and let it cool completely, then chill for at least 30 minutes until firm.

SOAK THE GELATIN LEAVES in cold water to cover for a few minutes until softened. Heat the shellfish stock until boiling, then remove from the heat and season well with salt and pepper. Drain the gelatin leaves and lightly squeeze out the excess water, then add to the hot stock, stirring until dissolved. Set the stock aside to cool slightly.

LIGHTLY OIL a 4-cup (1-L) terrine mould (or loaf pan), then line it with plastic wrap, letting the wrap hang over the sides of the pan.

USING A VERY SHARP KNIFE, slice the fish fillets and lobster into long strips about the same thickness as the langoustine tails. Ladle some shellfish stock into the lined mould, to coat the bottom thinly. Now arrange a mixture of fish and shellfish strips neatly over the bottom to form the first layer, uncurling the langoustine tails as you place them. Season lightly and scatter some chopped herbs on top. Pour in a little more stock and add another layer of fish, shellfish, seasoning, and herbs.

CONTINUE LAYERING in this way until you've used up all the fish and shellfish, then add a final ladleful of stock. Fold the plastic wrap over the mosaic to cover it, then place a small tray that fits snugly in the mould on top and weight down with a few cans of food. Chill the mosaic overnight until it has set.

FOR THE SAFFRON POTATOES, bring the vegetable stock to a boil with the saffron and 1 tsp (5 mL) sea salt added. Peel the potatoes and cut into slices ½ inch (1 cm) thick. Add them to the stock and simmer until just tender but still holding their shape, 4–5 minutes. Drain well and pat dry with paper towels. Cut the potatoes into neat cubes, place them in a bowl, and pour the vinaigrette over. Toss the potatoes carefully to coat in the dressing, then set aside to infuse for 5–10 minutes, while you unmould the mosaic.

TO UNMOULD THE MOSAIC, peel back the plastic wrap covering the terrine and carefully turn over onto a board. Lift off the mould and remove the plastic wrap. Using a serrated knife, cut the mosaic into slices ⅝ inch (1.5 cm) thick. Lift a slice onto each serving plate, using a spatula, then gently rub a little olive oil over the surface to give a shiny glaze.

TO SERVE, arrange the sliced carrots, onion rings, and saffron potatoes around each plate. Carefully pour a thin layer of chilled tomato consommé over the top. Garnish with a few snipped chives and tiny sprigs of chervil, tarragon, and dillweed. Finally, spoon a neat quenelle of caviar, if using, on top of the mosaic slices and serve at once.

Ravioli of lobster, langoustine, and salmon with a lemongrass and chervil velouté

THIS EXQUISITE APPETIZER IS A LONG-STANDING FAVOURITE. I LIKE TO INCLUDE SOME LANGOUSTINES IN THE FILLING, BUT TO SIMPLIFY THE RECIPE YOU CAN USE ALL LOBSTER MEAT, WITH A LITTLE SALMON MOUSSE TO BIND. MAKE THE RAVIOLI FILLING AND SHELLFISH STOCK A DAY IN ADVANCE. *[Illustrated on page 23]*

Serves 8 as an appetizer

RAVIOLI FILLING:
10 oz (300 g) skinned salmon fillet
Sea salt and black pepper
¼ cup (50 mL) whipping cream
10 oz (300 g) lobster meat (from 1 lobster tail and claws)
5 oz (150 g) langoustine meat (from 5–6 langoustines or scampi)
Squeeze of lemon juice
Handful of mixed herbs (basil, coriander, and chervil), chopped

RAVIOLI:
10 oz (300 g) saffron pasta dough (see page 250 – about ⅓ quantity)
1 egg yolk, beaten with a pinch of salt and 2 tsp (10 mL) water (egg wash)

FOR SERVING:
Reduced shellfish stock (see page 246), for drizzling
Lemongrass and chervil velouté (see page 248)
Buttered leaf spinach
Olive oil, for drizzling
½ cup (125 mL) tomato chutney (see page 250), optional
8 basil crisps (see page 248), optional

FIRST, MAKE THE RAVIOLI FILLING. Put one-third of the salmon into a food processor with some salt and pepper, and blend to a firm purée. With the motor running, slowly trickle in the cream. Transfer to a bowl, cover with plastic wrap, and chill for 20 minutes. Finely dice the lobster and langoustine meat and the remaining salmon fillet. Mix together in a bowl, then cover and chill for 20 minutes.

FOLD ENOUGH SALMON PURÉE into the diced lobster mixture to bind it, then add the lemon juice, chopped herbs, salt, and pepper. To check the seasoning, blanch a little spoonful of the filling, then taste it. Chill the mixture for 20 minutes until firm before shaping into 8 neat balls. Place on a plate, cover with plastic wrap, and chill until firm.

TO MAKE THE RAVIOLI, roll out the pasta dough into thin sheets, using a pasta machine. Transfer to a lightly floured surface and cut out 16 rounds of 5 inch (12 cm) diameter, using a pastry cutter. Place a ball of filling in the centre of half of the pasta rounds, then brush the edges with egg wash. Place another pasta round on top of each one and press the edges together to seal, stretching the dough slightly and moulding it around the filling with your fingers to make sure there are no air gaps. Use a pair of kitchen scissors to cut around the ravioli to neaten the edges.

BLANCH THE RAVIOLI in boiling salted water for 3–4 minutes, then refresh in ice water. Remove with a slotted spoon and place on a tray. Cover with plastic wrap and refrigerate until ready to serve.

WHEN READY TO SERVE, warm up the reduced shellfish stock. Reheat the lemongrass velouté, adding the chopped chervil as you take the pan off the heat. Add the ravioli to a large pan of boiling salted water and boil for 2–3 minutes to reheat. Remove with a slotted spoon and drain well.

DRIZZLE A SPIRAL of shellfish stock around each warm plate. Spoon a little warm spinach into the centre and place a ravioli on top. Drizzle a little olive oil over and top with a quenelle of tomato chutney and a basil crisp, if you like. Pour the lemongrass and chervil velouté over or pass around separately.

Salad of lobster with octopus carpaccio, roasted watermelon, baby squid, and a shellfish sauce

THIS MAY SEEM AN UNLIKELY COMBINATION, BUT THE FLAVOURS WORK WELL TOGETHER. OCTOPUS CARPACCIO IS QUITE TIME-CONSUMING TO PREPARE AND NEEDS TO BE MADE A DAY AHEAD. FOR A SIMPLER PRESENTATION, ARRANGE THE SALAD ON A BED OF MIXED LEAVES DRESSED WITH A LIGHT VINAIGRETTE. *[Illustrated on page 25]*

Serves 4 as an appetizer

OCTOPUS CARPACCIO:

1 octopus, cleaned
Few thyme sprigs
1 bay leaf
½ head of garlic, split horizontally (unpeeled)
Sea salt and black pepper

DEEP-FRIED SQUID:

7 oz (200 g) baby squid, cleaned
Peanut or vegetable oil, for deep-frying
2–3 tbsp (30–45 mL) all-purpose flour, for dusting
½ quantity tempura batter (see page 251)

SHELLFISH SAUCE:

1 large shallot, peeled and finely chopped
4 tsp (20 mL) butter
⅔ cup (150 mL) Noilly Prat (or other dry vermouth)
1¼ cups (300 mL) shellfish stock (see page 246)
⅔ cup (150mL) whipping cream

LOBSTER SALAD:

2–3 large slices of ripe watermelon, about ⅝ inch (1.5 cm) thick
2 tbsp (30 mL) olive oil
2 cooked lobster tails, shelled

FOR SERVING:

Olive oil, for drizzling
Handful of mixed herb salad
1–2 baby romaine hearts

FIRST, PREPARE THE OCTOPUS. Put it in a large pot with the herbs, garlic, and some salt and pepper. Pour in enough water to cover. Bring to a boil, then lower the heat to a simmer and cook until tender, 1–2 hours. To test, pierce the "skirt" (the thickest part of the octopus where the head connects to the tentacles) with a sharp knife.

RUB OFF THE SKIN of the octopus while still hot, wearing rubber gloves to protect your hands. If it starts to cool down, dip it briefly in the hot poaching water—it's much easier to remove the skin when hot. Cut off the tentacles and discard the head (or use in another dish).

LINE A 4-CUP (1-L) LOAF PAN or cake pan with lightly oiled plastic wrap, letting plenty of excess hang over the sides. Working fast, trim the tentacles and arrange in the loaf pan, packing them in tightly so there is little space between them. Fold the excess wrap over to cover the octopus, then weight down by placing a similar-sized loaf pan or a small metal tray and a few cans of food on top. (The gelatinous texture of the octopus will make the tentacles stick together as long as they are pressed while still warm.) Chill the octopus overnight until firm.

TO PREPARE THE SQUID, cut the pouches into small rings, keeping the tentacles whole. Pat dry with paper towels and refrigerate.

FOR THE SHELLFISH SAUCE, sweat the shallot in a saucepan with the butter and some seasoning, stirring occasionally, until soft but not browned, 6–8 minutes. Add the vermouth, scraping the bottom of the pan to deglaze. Boil until reduced right down, then pour in the stock. Cook until the liquid has reduced again by half. Pour in the cream and let bubble until the sauce is the consistency of thick but pourable cream. Taste and adjust the seasoning, then strain through a fine sieve into a clean pan. Set aside.

WHEN READY TO SERVE, unmould the octopus from the pan and remove the plastic wrap. Using a very sharp knife, slice across the tentacles as thinly as possible. Arrange 3 or 4 slices on each serving plate to form a neat rectangle. Rub a little olive oil over the octopus carpaccio to give it a shiny appearance. Sprinkle with a little sea salt and set aside while you prepare the rest of the salad.

TO DEEP-FRY THE SQUID, heat the oil in a deep-fryer or saucepan to 350°F (180°C): A piece of bread should sizzle immediately when dropped into the hot oil. Toss the squid in the flour to coat and shake off any excess. Working in batches, draw the squid through the tempura batter and carefully add to the hot oil. Deep-fry for a few minutes until the batter is lightly golden and crisp. Drain on paper towels, and repeat with the remaining squid. Keep warm in a low oven.

FOR THE LOBSTER SALAD, cut the watermelon into 1½-inch (4-cm) rounds with a pastry cutter. Heat up a skillet and add a little olive oil. Season the lobster tails and briefly sear in the hot skillet over high heat, turning frequently, until lightly golden. Remove to a plate and let rest. Add a little more oil to the skillet and fry the watermelon rounds for 1–2 minutes on each side until they are lightly caramelized.

TO ASSEMBLE, gently warm the shellfish sauce. Slice the lobster tails into rounds ⅝ inch (1.5 cm) thick. Arrange the lobster and watermelon slices, overlapping, on each plate, diagonally across the octopus carpaccio. Top the lobster slices with the deep-fried squid tentacles and arrange the crisp squid rings around the plate. Garnish with the salad leaves and lettuce hearts, then drizzle a little olive oil over. Serve the shellfish sauce alongside.

Seared loin of tuna with poached veal filet, spring truffles, and caper dressing

I LOVE THE SIMPLICITY OF THIS APPETIZER–LEAN VEAL AND TUNA WITH SLICES OF FRAGRANT WHITE TRUFFLE AND A PIQUANT CAPER DRESSING. POACH THE VEAL, SEAR THE TUNA, AND PREPARE THE SAUCE WELL AHEAD, AND IT WILL TAKE YOU ONLY MINUTES TO ASSEMBLE THE DISH TO SERVE. *[Illustrated on page 28]*

Serves 6–8 as an appetizer

VEAL:
1 veal filet (tenderloin), preferably from the thick end, about 1¼ lb (625 g)
2 cups (500 mL) olive oil (approx)
Few thyme sprigs
2 garlic cloves, peeled
Sea salt and black pepper

TUNA:
1¼ lb (625 g) very fresh centre-cut tuna, ideally sashimi-grade
Drizzle of olive oil

CAPER DRESSING:
2 tbsp (30 mL) olive oil, plus extra for drizzling
1½ tbsp (25 mL) capers, rinsed and drained
1 small garlic clove, peeled and minced
1–2 tbsp (15–30 mL) lemon juice
1 cup (250 mL) mayonnaise (see page 249)
2 green onions, finely chopped

FOR SERVING:
1–2 white truffles, thinly sliced
2–3 tbsp (30–45 mL) capers, rinsed and drained
Mixed herb salad, lightly dressed with classic vinaigrette (see page 249)

TO PREPARE THE VEAL, cut off any fat or sinew surrounding the meat, then trim it to a neat round log that is about 2 inches (5 cm) thick. Wrap tightly with plastic wrap and chill for a few hours to set the shape.

TO PREPARE THE TUNA, trim to a neat log, similar in thickness to the veal filet. Save 3–4 oz (about 100 g) of the tuna trimmings for the dressing (use the rest for another dish). Wrap the tuna log tightly in plastic wrap and chill for 2–3 hours until firm.

POUR THE OLIVE OIL into a pot that is just large enough to hold the veal. Add the thyme and garlic and heat gently until just below simmering. Unwrap the veal and season all over with salt and pepper. Add to the pot, making sure that it is entirely submerged in the oil. Add a little more oil, if necessary. Cook gently for 15–20 minutes. For medium rare, the veal should feel slightly springy when pressed.

LIFT OUT THE VEAL onto a board, using a pair of tongs. Let cool completely. Wipe off any excess oil with paper towels, then wrap the veal tightly in plastic wrap and refrigerate until ready to serve.

HEAT A SKILLET until you can feel the heat rising above it. Unwrap the tuna and season with salt and pepper. Drizzle a little olive oil into the pan, then add the tuna. Roll it around the pan until it is evenly seared; this should only take 15–20 seconds on each side. Cool, then rewrap in plastic wrap and freeze until firm, 1½–2 hours.

FOR THE CAPER DRESSING, season the reserved tuna trimmings and quickly sear in a hot pan with a drizzle of olive oil. While still hot, place in a food processor with the capers, garlic, 2 tbsp (30 mL) olive oil, and 1 tbsp (15 mL) lemon juice. Blend to a smooth paste, stopping to scrape down the sides of the food processor once or twice. Add the mayonnaise and blitz again to combine. The dressing should be the consistency of thick but pourable cream; if it is too thick, add a little hot water and blend again. Transfer to a bowl and stir in the green onions. Taste and adjust the seasoning with salt, pepper, and a little more lemon juice, if required. Refrigerate if making in advance.

REMOVE THE TUNA from the freezer 10–15 minutes before you want to serve. Slice the tuna and veal as thinly as possible, using a very sharp knife. Let stand for a few minutes, so that the tuna is not frozen around the edges. Bring the dressing to room temperature.

TO SERVE, arrange the veal and tuna slices, overlapping them with the truffle slices in a circular fashion, on a platter or individual plates. Arrange the capers to form a border around the plate(s), then place a neat handful of mixed herb salad in the centre. Pour the dressing over just as you are about to serve.

Carpaccio of tuna and swordfish with a mixed herb salad and brown butter dressing

THIS EYE-CATCHING DISH IS MUCH EASIER THAN IT MIGHT APPEAR TO BE. PREPARE THE FISH AND MARINATE THE DAIKON WELL IN ADVANCE, LEAVING THE DRESSING UNTIL AN HOUR OR SO BEFORE SERVING. OBVIOUSLY YOU NEED TO USE VERY FRESH FISH IN PRIME CONDITION. *[Illustrated on page 29]*

Serves 4–6 as an appetizer

CARPACCIO:

1¼ lb (625 g) centre-cut loin of blue-fin tuna, ideally sashimi-grade

1¼ lb (625 g) centre-cut swordfish fillets

MARINATED DAIKON:

3 tbsp (45 mL) toasted sesame oil

1 tbsp (15 mL) olive oil

1 shallot, peeled and finely chopped

3 tbsp (45 mL) light soy sauce

3 tbsp (45 mL) balsamic vinegar

½ daikon (white radish), thicker end only

BROWN BUTTER DRESSING:

½ cup (125 mL) unsalted butter

Juice of 1 small lemon

Pinch of fine sea salt

4 tbsp (60 mL) whipping cream

Drizzle of olive oil

FOR SERVING:

Olive oil, for drizzling

Sea salt, for sprinkling

Baby chard leaves, for garnish

Oscietra caviar (optional)

FOR THE CARPACCIO, put the tuna and swordfish in the freezer 1–2 hours before preparing. This will make them easier to cut neatly.

TRIM THE TUNA and cut out 2 equal-sized square logs, each about 1 inch (2.5 cm) across. Remove the skin from the swordfish and cut out 2 square logs, similar to the width and length of the tuna logs. For optimum presentation, avoid including any brown or blood-tinged meat from the swordfish. (Use these and any trimmings from the tuna for another dish.)

PLACE THE TUNA AND SWORDFISH logs on a large piece of plastic wrap, alternately, to form a neat row. Trim both ends slightly to even up the logs, then wrap tightly in the plastic. Slide the fish onto a baking sheet and freeze until very firm, about 3 hours.

FOR THE MARINATED DAIKON, heat the sesame and olive oils, shallot, soy sauce, and balsamic vinegar in a small saucepan until bubbling. Take the pan off the heat and let cool to room temperature. Peel the daikon and thinly slice it lengthwise, using a mandoline. Pick out 12–14 neat slices and arrange them on one or two baking sheets in a single layer. Spread the shallot dressing over the sliced daikon. Wrap the trays with plastic wrap and let marinate at room temperature for 1½–2 hours.

FOR THE BROWN BUTTER DRESSING, gently melt the butter in a saucepan, then increase the heat and cook until golden brown. (Don't leave unattended as it will quickly burn.) As soon as it colours, take it off the heat and let stand for a few minutes. Pour off the clear liquid into a heatproof bowl, leaving the sediment behind. Cool to room temperature.

POUR THE LEMON JUICE into a food processor and add a generous pinch of salt. Pulse for a few seconds, then pour in the brown butter, cream, olive oil, and 3 tbsp (45 mL) boiling water. Blitz to emulsify for 10–15 seconds until you have a thick, creamy sauce. If it is too thick, add a little more boiling water and pulse again, stopping once to scrape down the sides of the processor. Transfer to a clean squeezy bottle and stand it in a pan of lukewarm water.

WHEN READY TO SERVE, unwrap the fish and slice across the logs into thin strips, using a long sharp knife. (At the restaurant, we use a meat slicer for this.)

SCRAPE OFF THE SHALLOTS from the marinated daikon, then cut the daikon into strips ½ inch (1 cm) thick and trim to neaten.

TO PLATE, carefully lift the fish strips with a knife and arrange on individual square plates to form a checkerboard pattern. Rub the fish with a little olive oil and sprinkle with some sea salt.

FORM A NEAT BORDER of daikon strips around the edge of the checkerboard, overlapping them as necessary. Pipe the brown butter dressing neatly around the inner edge of the daikon and garnish with baby chard leaves. Place a few tiny spoonfuls of caviar on the checkerboard to finish, if you like.

Fillet of red mullet with cod, green onion, and pearl barley risotto, and a sweet and sour pepper sauce

I LOVE THIS PRESENTATION, THOUGH IT RELIES ON USING ONLY THE TAIL HALF OF THE MULLET. IN THE RESTAURANT, WE USE THE REST OF THE FISH IN ANOTHER DISH. YOU CAN EITHER DO THE SAME OR USE 3 FILLETED RED MULLET INSTEAD. OMIT THE STUFFED LETTUCE BALLS FOR A SIMPLER DISH. *[Illustrated on page 31]*

Serves 6 as an appetizer

6 small red mullet, tail half only (see above)
Pinch of saffron strands
Olive oil, for drizzling
Sea salt and black pepper

SWEET AND SOUR PEPPER SAUCE:
1 tbsp (15 mL) olive oil
2 shallots, peeled and chopped
1/2 head of garlic, split horizontally (unpeeled)
1/2 tsp (2 mL) coriander seeds
2 red sweet peppers, cored, seeded, and chopped
1/2 yellow sweet pepper, cored, seeded, and chopped
Few tarragon sprigs, roughly chopped
4 tbsp (60 mL) white wine vinegar
1 cup (250 mL) Noilly Prat (or other dry vermouth)
1 cup (250 mL) vegetable stock (see page 247)
4 tsp (20 mL) butter, diced

STUFFED LETTUCE BALLS:
24 outer leaves from 4 heads baby romaine lettuce, cores trimmed
1 skinless, boneless chicken breast half, about 4 oz (125 g), chopped
1 tbsp (15 mL) lemon juice
2 tbsp (30 mL) whipping cream
Scant 2 oz (50 g) foie gras

RISOTTO:
4 cups (1 L) fish stock (see page 246)
Few thyme sprigs, 1 bay leaf
Scant 4 oz (100 g) cod fillet, with skin
1 cup (250 mL) pearl barley
4 tsp (20 mL) butter, diced
2 tbsp (30 mL) mascarpone
3 tbsp (45 mL) freshly grated parmesan
2 green onions, finely sliced

FOR SERVING:
Sautéed red and yellow sweet peppers
1 tbsp (15 mL) tapenade (see page 249), mixed with 1/4 cup (50 mL) olive oil

TO PREPARE THE RED MULLET, remove the lower fin. Now, without cutting through the top fin, use a sharp fish knife to cut along and around the backbone, then snap the end connecting to the tail to remove the bone. You want to keep the top flesh and tail intact so that the fish opens out like a butterfly. Trim off the top fin with scissors and pull out any pin bones with tweezers. Trim the fish slightly to neaten the edges.

MIX THE SAFFRON with a generous drizzle of olive oil in a large bowl. Toss the fish in the oil to coat, then open out the fillets and lay them, flesh side down, on a rimmed baking sheet. Cover with plastic wrap and refrigerate.

TO MAKE THE SAUCE, heat the olive oil in a pan and sweat the shallots with the garlic and coriander seeds until beginning to soften but not brown, about 5 minutes. Add the sweet peppers and tarragon and stir over high heat for 3–4 minutes. Add the wine vinegar, scraping the bottom of the pan to deglaze. Let bubble until reduced right down and the pan is quite dry. Pour in the vermouth and boil to reduce by two-thirds. Pour in the stock and boil until reduced by half. Discard the garlic, then tip the contents of the pan into a food processor. Pulse for a few seconds to a rough purée, then strain the sauce through a cheesecloth-lined sieve into a clean pan. Adjust the seasoning, adding 1 tsp (5 mL) sugar to balance the acidity, if required. Set aside.

FOR THE STUFFED LETTUCE BALLS, blanch the lettuce leaves in boiling water for a few seconds until just wilted but still bright green. Immediately drain and refresh in a bowl of ice water, then pat dry with a clean kitchen towel. Put the chicken in a food processor with the lemon juice and some seasoning. Blend to a thick paste, scraping down the sides of the processor once or twice. With the motor running, slowly pour in the cream. Add the foie gras and blitz to combine. To check the seasoning, blanch a little spoonful, then taste. Transfer the filling to a bowl, cover with plastic wrap, and chill for 20–30 minutes until firm.

LAY TWO LETTUCE LEAVES on a piece of plastic wrap, overlapping them slightly. Roll a tablespoonful of the chicken filling into a ball and place in the middle. Fold the leaves to enclose the filling and form a neat ball. Wrap tightly in the plastic wrap. Repeat with the rest of the filling and lettuce leaves. Keep the stuffed lettuce balls refrigerated until ready to serve.

FOR THE RISOTTO, heat 1¼ cups (300 mL) of the fish stock with the herbs in a wide pan until just simmering. Season the cod and poach in the stock until the flesh is opaque and just cooked, 3–4 minutes. Lift out and let cool slightly, then flake the fish, discarding the skin and pin bones. Strain the stock and set aside with the cod.

PUT THE PEARL BARLEY in a pan with the rest of the fish stock and bring to a boil. Simmer, stirring from time to time, until tender, 40–45 minutes. Remove from the heat and set aside.

TO FINISH THE RISOTTO, reheat the barley in a saucepan with the reserved stock until most of the stock is absorbed. Gradually stir in the butter to give the barley grains a glossy shine. Add the mascarpone, parmesan, and salt and pepper to taste. Take off the heat and mix in the green onions and cod. Keep warm.

POACH THE LETTUCE BALLS in a pot of boiling salted water for 4 minutes; remove with a slotted spoon and drain on paper towels. Reheat the sweet and sour sauce and slowly whisk in the butter.

SEASON THE RED MULLET and fry, skin side down, in a hot non-stick skillet until the skin is crisp and the fish is cooked two-thirds of the way through, 1½–2 minutes. (As the fish is coated in saffron oil, you don't need to add oil to the pan.) Turn and cook the flesh side for 30 seconds only.

TO SERVE, ladle some barley risotto into the middle of each warm plate and place a red mullet on top, skin side up. Arrange 2 stuffed lettuce balls and a few sautéed peppers alongside. Drizzle the tapenade dressing around the plates and spoon on the sweet and sour pepper sauce.

Ballotine of foie gras with Label Anglais chicken, marinated shimeji mushrooms, and a port vinaigrette

THE CHICKEN AND MARINATED SHIMEJI MUSHROOMS CUT THE RICHNESS OF THE FOIE GRAS IN THIS STYLISH APPETIZER. YOU WILL NEED TO ORDER GRADE-A FOIE GRAS IN ADVANCE FROM A QUALITY BUTCHER, AND START THIS DISH A DAY AHEAD. TAKE GREAT CARE TO AVOID OVERCOOKING THE BALLOTINE. *[Illustrated on page 35]*

Serves 8–10 as an appetizer

BALLOTINE:
1 cup (250 mL) clarified butter (see clarify, page 252)
Few thyme sprigs
Few rosemary sprigs
3 garlic cloves, peeled
4 skinless, boneless chicken breast halves (preferably Label Anglais), about 4 oz (125 g) each
Sea salt and black pepper
2 tbsp (30 mL) sliced almonds, lightly toasted
⅓ cup (75 mL) truffle-infused Madeira sauce (see page 248)
1 whole duck or goose foie gras, about 1 lb 6 oz (700 g)
Large pinch of pink salt
1 tbsp (15 mL) sweet wine reduction (see page 152)
2 oz (50–60 g) truffle shavings or trimmings, minced (optional)

MARINATED SHIMEJI MUSHROOMS:
4 oz (125 g) baby shimeji mushrooms, bases trimmed
1½ tbsp (25 mL) olive oil
1 tbsp (15 mL) sherry vinegar
2 tbsp (30 mL) hazelnut oil

CAULIFLOWER BASE:
¼ head of cauliflower, trimmed and finely chopped
Handful of flat-leaf parsley and chervil leaves, finely chopped
Scant 2 oz (50 g) shallot confit (see page 250)
4–5 tbsp (60–75 mL) classic vinaigrette (see page 249)

FOR SERVING:
Handful of small watercress sprigs
Drizzle of port vinaigrette (see page 249)
Pan-grilled or barbecued rosemary focaccia

TO MAKE THE BALLOTINE, first prepare the chicken filling. Put the clarified butter, herbs, and garlic in a medium pan. Gently heat the butter without letting it boil; there should be very little movement in the liquid. Season the chicken breasts with salt and pepper and place in the pan in a single layer, making sure that they are well coated with the butter. Slowly cook the chicken for about 45 minutes, regulating the heat to insure that the temperature remains constantly low. The chicken breasts should feel firm when cooked.

LET THE CHICKEN COOL SLIGHTLY in the butter, then drain and cut into thin slices. While still warm, put the chicken slices into a bowl with the sliced almonds and truffle Madeira sauce. Mix well and let cool slightly. Spread a few layers of plastic wrap on a work surface. Spoon the chicken mixture in a row along the lower third of the plastic. Fold over the bottom and sides of the plastic to cover, then roll up the chicken mixture into a tight log about 1½–2 inches (4–5 cm) in diameter. Try to avoid any large air bubbles in the log. Chill for 4 hours or overnight until firm.

TO PREPARE THE FOIE GRAS, carefully separate the lobes into two halves and remove the central vein and any large connecting membranes with a small sharp knife. Try to keep the liver as intact as possible, but take out any blood spots with the tip of the knife.

SPREAD TWO SHEETS OF PLASTIC WRAP on the work surface, overlapping the sides to make a large rectangle. Press the foie gras onto the plastic, shaping it into a rectangle wide and long enough to wrap around the chicken log. Sprinkle all over with the pink salt, pepper, and sweet wine reduction.

UNWRAP THE CHICKEN LOG and place in the centre of the foie gras. Use the ends of the plastic wrap to roll up the log, making sure the foie gras evenly covers the chicken log and there are no large air pockets in between. Use more plastic wrap to wrap the log tightly, then chill for a few hours until firm.

HALF-FILL A LARGE PAN or roasting pan with water and heat until the water temperature reaches 150°F (65°C) on a cooking thermometer. Lower the ballotine into the water and cook for 8–10 minutes at this temperature. (Use a heat diffuser under the pan to make it easier to control the heat.) Remove the ballotine and pat dry. Roll the log on a work surface to reshape it, then chill for a few hours until firm.

IF USING, SCATTER the chopped truffle trimmings on a large rimless baking sheet to form an even layer and roll the ballotine over them to coat. Rewrap the truffle-coated ballotine in plastic wrap and chill until ready to serve.

SAUTÉ THE SHIMEJI MUSHROOMS in a hot pan with the olive oil and seasoning over high heat for 2–3 minutes. Take the pan off the heat and immediately dress the mushrooms with the sherry vinegar and hazelnut oil. (They can be left to marinate overnight, if you want to prepare the mushrooms in advance.)

TO SERVE, mix all the ingredients for the cauliflower base together and season well with salt and pepper. Spoon a thin layer into a round metal cutter placed in the centre of a serving plate, then remove the cutter. Cut a slice ⅝ inch (1.5 cm) thick from the foie gras ballotine and place on top of the cauliflower base. Repeat for the other serving plates.

GARNISH THE PLATES with the marinated mushrooms and watercress leaves. Finally, add a drizzle of port vinaigrette. Serve with focaccia.

Pressed foie gras with Sauternes and chamomile jelly

WE SERVE THIS DECADENT APPETIZER WITH BRIOCHE FLAVOURED WITH FRESH TRUFFLE IN THE RESTAURANT. AS AN ALTERNATIVE, YOU COULD SERVE LIGHTLY TOASTED BRIOCHE SLICES DRIZZLED WITH TRUFFLE OIL. REMEMBER TO ORDER GRADE-A FOIE GRAS FROM A QUALITY BUTCHER IN ADVANCE. *[Illustrated on page 36]*

Serves 8–9 as an appetizer

SWEET WINE REDUCTION:

¼ cup (50 mL) white port
¼ cup (50 mL) sweet dessert wine (such as Sauternes or Montbazillac)
¼ cup (50 mL) brandy
1 thyme sprig
1 rosemary sprig

FOIE GRAS:

1 whole fresh duck or goose foie gras, about 1½ lb (700–750 g)
Pinch of pink sea salt
Sea salt and black pepper

CHAMOMILE JELLY:

1 heaped tsp (heaped 5 mL) chamomile tea leaves (or 1 chamomile tea bag)
⅓ cup (75 mL) granulated sugar
4 sheets of leaf gelatin (½ oz/15 g)
2 cups (500 mL) Sauternes

VEGETABLES À LA GREQUE:

1 head of baby cauliflower, cut into small florets
2 baby onions, peeled, sliced, and separated into rings
Scant 2 oz (50 g) fine green beans, blanched
7 tbsp (105 mL) olive oil
2 tbsp (30 mL) white wine vinegar
½ tsp (2 mL) coriander seeds
½ tsp (2 mL) white peppercorns
1 tsp (5 mL) granulated sugar (optional)
Scant 4 oz (100 g) shimeji mushrooms, trimmed
4 radishes, trimmed and halved

FOR SERVING:

Flat-leaf parsley crisps (see page 248), optional

FIRST MAKE THE WINE REDUCTION. Put all the ingredients into a small saucepan and boil until reduced by half. Set aside to cool to room temperature.

FOR THE FOIE GRAS, take it out of the fridge 1–2 hours before preparing and let it soften at room temperature. This will make it easier to handle.

TO PREPARE THE FOIE GRAS, carefully separate the lobes into two halves and remove the central vein and any large connecting membranes with a small sharp knife and kitchen tweezers. Try to keep the liver as intact as possible, but take out any blood spots with the tip of the knife. Place the foie gras in a bowl, sprinkle with sea salt, and pour the sweet wine reduction over the top. Cover the bowl with plastic wrap and chill for a few hours or overnight.

REMOVE THE FOIE GRAS from the fridge an hour before cooking. Line an 8-cup (2-L) loaf pan with parchment paper. Preheat the oven to 200°F (100°C). Sprinkle a little pink salt over the bottom of the pan, then pack in the foie gras, seasoning as you go. If necessary, cut any thick pieces in half horizontally, to even out the thickness of the terrine. Try to avoid gaps between the slices. Cut a sheet of waxed paper to cover the foie gras, then use a slightly smaller loaf pan (or a piece of cardboard cut to the size of the pan) to press down and flatten the liver. Remove the pan (or cardboard).

LAY A KITCHEN TOWEL over the bottom of a deep roasting pan and set the loaf pan on top. The towel will prevent direct contact with the roasting pan and help to insure that the foie gras cooks gently and evenly. Pour enough hot water into the roasting pan to come halfway up the sides of the loaf pan, then cover it with a piece of foil. Place in the oven and bake for about 45 minutes. Remove the pan from the water bath and let cool completely. Place the smaller pan or piece of cardboard on top of the foie gras and weight down with one or two cans of food. Chill overnight until firm.

FOR THE CHAMOMILE JELLY, place the chamomile tea and sugar in a measuring cup and pour in 1 cup (250 mL) boiling water. Stir to dissolve the sugar, then let the tea infuse for 15–20 minutes.

MEANWHILE SOAK THE GELATIN in cold water to cover for a few minutes until softened. Boil the Sauternes in a saucepan until reduced by half. Strain the chamomile tea into a metal bowl and add the Sauternes. Drain the gelatin leaves and squeeze out excess water, then add to the chamomile and Sauternes mixture; stir until dissolved.

SET THE BOWL in a larger bowl filled with ice water and set aside. Whisk the chamomile mixture from time to time as it cools. Fit a pastry bag with a large plain tip and seal the end with a small piece of plastic wrap.

WHEN THE JELLY HAS LIGHTLY SET (it will have a soft, loose texture), after about 1½–2 hours, spoon it into the pastry bag. Secure the end with a rubber band and refrigerate until ready to serve.

FOR THE VEGETABLES À LA GREQUE, blanch the cauliflower, onions, and beans separately in boiling salted water for 2–3 minutes each until just tender, then refresh in cold water and drain well. Put the olive oil, wine vinegar, coriander seeds, peppercorns, and sugar, if using, in a small saucepan and bring to a boil. Add the blanched vegetables and simmer for 1–2 minutes. Tip in the mushrooms and radishes and immediately remove the pan from the heat. Season with salt and pepper to taste and let cool to room temperature, about 15–20 minutes.

TO SERVE, unmould the foie gras terrine by carefully pulling out the parchment paper. Trim off some of the yellow fat from the top of the terrine, if you prefer. Using a warm knife, cut the terrine into batons ¾ inch (2 cm) thick, and trim off the sides to neaten. Place two batons on each serving plate, leaving a ¾ inch (2 cm) gap in between them. Pipe the jelly in between the foie gras batons. Arrange the vegetables à la greque in neat rows on both sides of the foie gras. Garnish with parsley crisps, if using, and drizzle a little olive oil around the plate. Serve with slices of truffle brioche or thin toast.

Fricassée of snails with spinach, baby artichokes, mushrooms, pancetta, and Jerusalem artichoke purée

THIS NOVEL APPROACH TO COOKING SNAILS TAKES A LITTLE TIME. OUR SNAILS COME PRE-COOKED AND SHELLED, BUT WE THEN GENTLY CONFIT THEM WITH CARAMELIZED SHALLOTS AND ARMAGNAC, WHICH GIVES THEM SWEETNESS AND A DISTINCT NUTTINESS—PERFECT WITH THE JERUSALEM ARTICHOKE PURÉE. *[Illustrated on page 38]*

Serves 6 as an appetizer

SNAILS:
2 tbsp (30 mL) olive oil
2 large shallots, peeled and finely chopped
3 garlic cloves, peeled and finely chopped
8 oz (250 g) shelled snails (pre-boiled for 3 minutes)
¼ cup (50 mL) packed dark brown sugar
1 tbsp (30 mL) tomato paste
¼ cup (50 mL) Armagnac
¼ cup (50 mL) slivered almonds
Sea salt and black pepper
1–1¼ cups (250–300 mL) melted butter

JERUSALEM ARTICHOKE PURÉE:
14 oz (400 g) Jerusalem artichokes, washed
4 cups (1 L) whole milk
3 tbsp (45 mL) butter, diced
7 tbsp (105 mL) whipping cream

FRICASSÉE:
30 baby artichokes
Juice of 1 lemon
3¼ cups (800 mL) vegetable stock (see page 247)
1 bay leaf
Few thyme sprigs
2 tbsp (30 mL) olive oil
10 oz (300 g) mixed mushrooms (such as morels and cèpes), cleaned and halved if large
1–2 tbsp (15–30 mL) butter, diced

FOR SERVING:
Handful of baby spinach leaves, washed
1–2 black truffles, thinly sliced (optional)
Garlic purée (see page 250)
Flat-leaf parsley crisps (see page 248), optional

TO COOK THE SNAILS, heat the olive oil in a small saucepan and add the shallots and garlic. Stir over medium heat for 4–5 minutes until they begin to soften. Add the snails, sugar, and tomato paste and increase the heat slightly. Cook for 3–4 minutes, stirring frequently, until the shallots are slightly caramelized. Pour in the Armagnac, scraping the bottom of the pan with a wooden spoon to deglaze. Add the almonds and seasoning, then pour in enough butter to cover. Bring to a gentle simmer, then turn the heat to the lowest setting and partially cover with a lid. Gently cook the snails until tender, 3–4 hours, giving the mixture a stir occasionally. Tip into a fine sieve to drain off the excess butter before using.

FOR THE ARTICHOKE PURÉE, cut the Jerusalem artichokes into thin slices, leaving their skins on, and place in the pan with the milk and 1 tbsp (15 mL) of the butter. Cook for 12–15 minutes, stirring occasionally, until they are very soft and you can break them up with a wooden spoon. Drain, reserving the milk, and transfer to a food processor. Pour in half of the milk and blend for a few minutes until smooth.

PUSH THE PURÉE through a fine sieve back into the pan. Gently reheat and stir in the remaining butter and the cream. Stir in enough of the remaining milk to achieve a thick but pourable purée. Season well with salt and pepper to taste. (This purée can be made up to 2 days in advance and kept refrigerated.)

FOR THE FRICASSÉE, prepare the artichokes one at a time. First, add the lemon juice to a bowl of ice water. Cut away the tip of the artichoke and the tough outer leaves with a small sharp knife, until you reach the light green, tender leaves. Trim off the tough skin from the stalk and base, then drop the artichoke into the bowl of acidulated water. Repeat to prepare the rest.

BRING THE STOCK TO A BOIL in a large pan with the bay leaf and thyme sprigs added. Blanch the baby artichokes in the stock until tender when pierced with a fine skewer, 5–7 minutes. Lift out with a slotted spoon and let cool.

WHEN READY TO SERVE, cut the baby artichokes in half vertically. Heat a large sauté pan, then add the olive oil, followed by the artichokes. Season with salt and pepper and fry until the artichokes are golden brown at the edges. Remove from the pan and keep warm.

ADD THE MUSHROOMS and butter to the same pan and toss over high heat. Tip in the snails and toss well to mix. Sauté for a few minutes until the snails are warmed through and any liquid released by the mushrooms has evaporated. Remove the pan from the heat and keep warm. Reheat the artichoke purée.

TO ASSEMBLE, arrange the baby spinach in a circle around each serving plate, alternating each leaf with a slice of black truffle, if using. Dot the garlic purée around the edge of the plates. Place a deep metal cutter in the centre of each plate and squeeze a little more garlic purée over it. Arrange the artichoke halves around the inside of the cutters with the cut sides facing outward and stalk ends uppermost. Fill the middle with the snail and mushroom fricassée. Carefully lift up the metal cutters and add a parsley crisp garnish, if you like. Pour the Jerusalem artichoke purée around the spinach border and serve.

Tartare of beef filet with oscietra caviar and marinated red and yellow peppers

THE FIRST REQUIREMENT FOR A GOOD STEAK TARTARE IS THE FINEST FILET OF BEEF. CHILL IT WELL BEFORE DICING BY HAND, USING A RAZOR-SHARP KNIFE, AND AVOID OVERWORKING, SO IT RETAINS A CLEAN TEXTURE AND TASTE. THIS PRESENTATION IS STUNNING, BUT YOU CAN OMIT THE CAVIAR AND JUST USE PEPPERS FOR A LESS EXTRAVAGANT FINISH. *[Illustrated on page 41]*

Serves 4 as an appetizer

MARINATED PEPPERS:
1 red sweet pepper
1 yellow sweet pepper
2 garlic cloves, peeled and sliced
Few thyme sprigs
Sea salt and black pepper
Olive oil, for drizzling

TARTARE OF BEEF:
1¼ lb (625 g) filet of beef (tenderloin)
1 tbsp (15 mL) capers, rinsed, drained, and chopped
1 large shallot, peeled and finely chopped
1 green onion, finely chopped

DEEP-FRIED ONION RINGS:
2 small onions, peeled
1–2 tbsp (15–30mL) all-purpose flour, for dusting
½ quantity tempura batter (see page 251)
Peanut or vegetable oil, for deep-frying

FOR SERVING:
4 tbsp (60 mL) oscietra caviar, or to taste
8 blanched asparagus tips
1 roasted yellow sweet pepper, cut into neat squares
1–2 black truffles, cut into neat squares (optional)
Handful of capers, rinsed and drained
Olive oil, for drizzling

FIRST PREPARE THE MARINATED PEPPERS. Preheat the broiler. Quarter the peppers and remove the core and seeds. Place, skin side up, on a baking sheet and broil, close to the heat, until the skins have blackened and blistered, about 5 minutes. Tip into a bowl, cover with plastic wrap, and set aside for a few minutes (the steam trapped inside will help lift the skin).

UNCOVER AND PEEL off the skin, then finely chop the peppers and place in a bowl. Add the garlic, thyme, salt, pepper, and a generous drizzle of olive oil. Toss well, then cover and let marinate in a warm place for 1–1½ hours.

FOR THE TARTARE, trim the beef filet of any fat or sinew, then cut into thin slices. Cut each slice into strips, then gather the strips together a few at a time and cut across into very fine dice. Place in a bowl and add the capers, shallot, green onion, and some salt and pepper. Mix thoroughly until evenly combined, then taste and adjust the seasoning.

TO SHAPE THE TARTARE into patties, place a metal cutter on each serving plate and divide the beef tartare among them. Press down with the back of a spoon to level the meat, then tightly wrap each plate (with the metal ring still on top) in plastic wrap. Chill while you fry the onion rings.

FOR THE ONION RINGS, slice the onions into rings and pat dry. Heat the peanut oil in a deep-fryer or deep, heavy-based saucepan to 350°F (180°C), or until a piece of bread dropped into the hot oil browns in 40 seconds. Deep-fry the onions in batches: Lightly dust the onion rings with flour, tip them into a sieve, and shake off any excess, then draw the onions through the tempura batter and drop into the hot oil. Fry until light golden and crisp, turning once. Remove with a slotted spoon to a tray lined with paper towels. Sprinkle lightly with sea salt. Keep hot in a low oven while you deep-fry the rest of the onions.

TO SERVE, REMOVE THE PLASTIC WRAP from the beef. Cover one half of the tartare with oscietra caviar and the other half with the marinated peppers, then remove the cutters. Arrange the asparagus tips on top. Garnish the edge of the plates with the yellow peppers, truffle, if using, and capers. Drizzle with a little olive oil and serve, accompanied by the hot, crisp onion rings.

Salad of asparagus, baby artichokes, and Perigord truffles with a creamy truffle dressing

THIS DRAMATIC PRESENTATION IS ACHIEVED BY SETTING THE ASPARAGUS SALAD IN DEEP METAL CUTTERS TO RESEMBLE CROWNS. IT LOOKS IMPRESSIVE, BUT YOU CAN SIMPLY TOSS THE ASPARAGUS AND CRESS IN THE CREAMY DRESSING AND PILE IT INTO THE CENTRE OF THE PLATES, IF YOU PREFER. *[Illustrated on page 44]*

Serves 4–6 as an appetizer

MARINATED VEGETABLES:
1½ lemons
12 baby artichokes
⅓ cup (75 mL) white wine vinegar
1 head of spring garlic, cloves separated and peeled
Scant 4 oz (100 g) small cauliflower florets
Scant 2 oz (50 g) fine green beans, trimmed
2 medium carrots, peeled
1 tbsp (15 mL) olive oil
16 pink radishes, trimmed and halved
1 tsp (5 mL) coriander seeds, crushed
4 tbsp (60 ml) classic vinaigrette (see page 249)
1 tsp (5 mL) granulated sugar (optional)

TRUFFLE DRESSING:
¼ cup (50 mL) extra-virgin olive oil
¼ cup (50 mL) truffle-infused olive oil
2 tbsp (30 mL) white wine vinegar
1 tbsp (15 mL) wholegrain mustard
2 tbsp (30 mL) whipping cream
Sea salt and black pepper

ASPARAGUS SALAD:
1½ lb (750 g) medium asparagus spears (about 32–36)
7 oz (200 g) mixed cress (such as baby chard leaves and pea shoots)

FOR SERVING:
Garlic purée (see page 250)
1 Perigord truffle, thinly sliced

FIRST, PREPARE THE MARINATED VEGETABLES. Add the juice of 1 lemon to a bowl of ice water. Prepare the artichokes one at a time: Cut away the tough outer leaves with a small sharp knife, until you reach the light green, tender leaves. Trim off the tough skin from the stalk and base of the artichoke. Trim the tip, then cut the head in half. Rub the cut surfaces with the lemon half, then immerse in the bowl of acidulated water while you prepare the rest.

ADD THE WINE VINEGAR to a medium saucepan of water and bring to a boil. Drop in the artichokes and simmer until tender when pierced with a fine skewer, 12–15 minutes, depending on size. Drain and pat dry with paper towels.

BRING A LARGE POT OF SALTED WATER to a boil, then add the garlic cloves, cauliflower, and green beans. Blanch the vegetables until tender-crisp, about 2 minutes. Remove from the pan with a slotted spoon and immediately refresh in ice water. Drain well, pat dry with paper towels, and set aside. Keep the pan of water on the heat.

USING A MANDOLINE (or a swivel vegetable peeler), slice the carrots lengthwise into ribbons. Blanch the carrot ribbons for 1 minute, then refresh in cold water and drain well.

HEAT THE OLIVE OIL in a large skillet and sauté the radishes with the crushed coriander until just softened, about 2–3 minutes. Stir in the blanched vegetables and artichokes and heat for 1–2 minutes. Add the vinaigrette, with the sugar if using, and stir for a few seconds. Season with salt and pepper to taste. Chill for at least 20 minutes before serving.

FOR THE TRUFFLE DRESSING, whisk all the ingredients together and season with salt and pepper to taste. Transfer to a jar or squeezy bottle and set aside.

TO PREPARE THE ASPARAGUS, break off the tough ends and peel the lower part of the stalks. Bring a pan of salted water to a boil. Add the asparagus spears and blanch until tender-crisp, about 2–3 minutes. Drain and immediately refresh in cold water. Drain and pat dry. Cut the asparagus spears in half lengthwise and trim the bases so the spears are the same length.

TO ASSEMBLE THE SALAD, put a deep round metal cutter in the centre of each serving plate. Put a little garlic purée around the moulds, then stand the asparagus spears upright inside them, alternating the cut and uncut sides facing outward. The thick garlic purée will act as a "glue" to help keep the asparagus spears upright. Put a small handful of mixed baby cress leaves inside each asparagus "crown."

TO FINISH THE PLATES, arrange the marinated vegetables around the edge, rolling up the carrot ribbons tightly. Top with the truffle slices. Carefully remove the metal cutters and drizzle the creamy truffle dressing over the asparagus "crowns" just before serving.

Pan-grilled asparagus with sel de Guérande, served with a tomato vinaigrette

SERVING ASPARAGUS VERY SIMPLY IS THE BEST WAY TO APPRECIATE ITS SUPERB FLAVOUR. A FRESH TOMATO VINAIGRETTE AND A LITTLE FLEUR DE SEL, FROM THE SALT MARSHES AROUND GUÉRANDE IN SOUTHWEST FRANCE, ARE ALL YOU NEED. *[Illustrated on page 45]*

Serves 4 as an appetizer

ASPARAGUS:
16 green asparagus spears, about 8 oz (250 g)
16 white asparagus spears, about 8 oz (250 g)
Olive oil, for drizzling
Few pinches of sel de Guérande
Sea salt and black pepper

TOMATO VINAIGRETTE:
2 ripe plum or roma tomatoes
½ cup (125 mL) extra-virgin olive oil
1 shallot, peeled and finely chopped
Juice of ½ lemon
1 tsp (5 mL) balsamic vinegar
1 tsp (5 mL) granulated sugar (optional)
Handful of large basil leaves, finely shredded

FOR SERVING:
12 large black olives, pitted, quartered, and trimmed
Tomato concassé (see page 248)
4 handfuls of mixed herb salad
Olive oil, for drizzling

BRING A POT OF SALTED WATER to a boil. Peel the asparagus spears using a swivel vegetable peeler, starting from just below the tip of each spear. Trim off the ends, so that the spears are more or less the same length. Blanch the asparagus for 1 minute, then immediately refresh in a bowl of ice water. Drain and pat dry with paper towels.

LAY THE ASPARAGUS SPEARS on a tray and drizzle with olive oil. Sprinkle with the sel de Guérande and some freshly ground black pepper and toss well to coat. Set aside until ready to cook.

FOR THE TOMATO VINAIGRETTE, put the tomatoes in a heatproof bowl, cover them with boiling water, and leave for 45–60 seconds to loosen their skins. Remove and peel away the skins. Cut the tomatoes into quarters, remove the seeds, and finely dice the flesh.

HEAT THE OLIVE OIL in a saucepan and sweat the shallot over low heat until softened, about 8–10 minutes. Add the lemon juice, diced tomatoes, balsamic vinegar, and sugar, if using. Increase the heat and cook until the tomatoes are soft, 5–7 minutes. Transfer to a food processor, add the shredded basil, and blitz to a purée. Season with salt and pepper to taste and keep warm.

HEAT A RIDGED CAST-IRON GRILL PAN until it is very hot and you can feel the heat rising. Add the asparagus spears and pan-grill for 2–3 minutes, turning occasionally, until they are slightly charred and just tender.

TO SERVE, arrange the asparagus on individual plates, alternating the green and white spears. Sprinkle lightly with a little more sel de Guérande. Neatly arrange the trimmed olives along each side, then place the tomato concassé in a diagonal line on top of the asparagus. Spoon a little more tomato concassé across the base of the spears, then pile a handful of mixed herb salad on top. Drizzle a little olive oil around the plate and spoon the tomato vinaigrette over the top as you serve.

Butternut squash velouté with sautéed cèpes, parmesan crisp, and mushroom and white truffle tortellini

CRISP GRATINÉED PARMESAN AND SAUTÉED CÈPES OFFSET THIS VELVETY SOUP PERFECTLY. IN THE RESTAURANT WE TAKE THE DISH TO NEW HEIGHTS BY GARNISHING IT WITH MUSHROOM AND WHITE TRUFFLE TORTELLINI AND SAUTÉED SCALLOPS, BUT YOU CAN LEAVE THESE OUT FOR A SIMPLER APPETIZER. *[Illustrated on page 48]*

Serves 4–6 as an appetizer

MUSHROOM AND WHITE TRUFFLE TORTELLINI:
⅓ quantity saffron pasta dough (see page 250)
2 tbsp (30 mL) butter
8 oz (250 g) cremino mushrooms, trimmed and finely chopped
Sea salt and black pepper
1 tsp (5 mL) truffle-infused olive oil
1 tbsp (15 mL) white truffle trimmings
2–3 tbsp (30–45 mL) mashed potato (enough to bind)
1 egg yolk, beaten with pinch of salt and 2 tsp (10 mL) water (egg wash)

BUTTERNUT SQUASH VELOUTÉ:
1 butternut squash, about 1½ lb (750 g)
3 tbsp (45 mL) olive oil
2 large shallots, peeled and finely chopped
2 tbsp (30 mL) butter
2½ cups (625 mL) hot vegetable stock (see page 247), approx
⅓ cup (75 mL) whipping cream

PARMESAN CRISP:
4–6 heaped tbsp (heaped 60–90 mL) grated parmesan
Black truffle trimmings and/or shavings

SAUTÉED CÈPES AND SCALLOPS:
1 tbsp (15 mL) olive oil
1–2 tbsp (15–30 mL) butter, diced
4 large fresh cèpes, thickly sliced
1 tbsp (15 mL) chopped flat-leaf parsley or chervil
2–3 sea scallops, shucked and cleaned

FOR SERVING:
Olive oil, for drizzling

FIRST, PREPARE THE TORTELLINI. Have the pasta dough ready and let it rest while you make the filling. Heat a sauté pan and add the butter and mushrooms. Season with salt and pepper and sauté over high heat for 5–7 minutes, stirring frequently. Evaporate any liquid released by the mushrooms. Transfer to a bowl and mix in the truffle-infused oil, truffle trimmings, and just enough mashed potato to bind the mixture. Taste and adjust the seasoning. Cover and chill for 30 minutes until firm, then roll the filling into 1-oz (30-g) balls and chill again.

TO SHAPE THE TORTELLINI, roll out the pasta thinly, using a pasta machine. Transfer to a lightly floured surface and stamp out discs using a 6-inch (15-cm) round cutter. Press a ball of mushroom filling onto one side of each pasta disc. Brush the pasta around the filling with egg wash, then fold the pasta over the filling to form semi-circles. Press the edges together to seal, making sure there are no air bubbles enclosed. Now curl the semi-circle around your little finger and press the tips together to form tortellini shapes (illustrated on page 49).

BLANCH THE TORTELLINI in boiling salted water for 2 minutes, then drain and refresh in a bowl of ice water. Drain again and lay out on an oiled tray. Wrap in plastic wrap and refrigerate.

FOR THE VELOUTÉ, peel and halve the butternut squash, remove the seeds, and chop the flesh. Heat the olive oil in a large saucepan and gently sauté the shallots until softened but not coloured, about 5 minutes. Tip in the squash and add the butter and some seasoning. Stir over medium-high heat until the squash is soft and lightly golden at the edges, 8–10 minutes. Pour in enough hot stock to cover and simmer until the squash is very soft, about 5 minutes.

TAKE THE PAN OFF THE HEAT and stir in the cream. Using a slotted spoon, scoop the vegetables into a blender. Add about one-third of the hot stock and blend until smooth. Press through a fine sieve into a clean pan. Stir in more of the hot stock until the squash velouté is a thick but pourable, creamy consistency. Check the seasoning and keep warm.

FOR THE PARMESAN CRISP, preheat the broiler. Heat a small non-stick skillet until hot. Scatter a heaped tablespoonful of parmesan in the pan to form an even layer, then sprinkle with a little truffle. When the sides begin to turn golden, flash the pan under the broiler, close to the heat, for a few seconds until the top is evenly golden. Remove the pan from the broiler and leave the parmesan crisp to firm up for about 30 seconds. Using a heatproof spatula, carefully peel the crisp off the pan and transfer to a tray to cool. Repeat with the rest of the parmesan.

WHEN READY TO SERVE, cook the cèpes: Heat the olive oil and butter in a skillet until the butter begins to foam. Season the cèpes and fry them, tossing occasionally, until golden brown around the edges, 2–3 minutes. Toss in the parsley and transfer to a warm plate.

HALVE EACH SCALLOP horizontally and season, then fry in the skillet for 1–1½ minutes on each side until golden brown and slightly springy when pressed. In the meantime, immerse the tortellini in a pan of boiling salted water and blanch for 2 minutes to warm through; drain well.

TO SERVE, rest a tortellini on a sautéed scallop disc on one side of each warm soup plate, then ladle the squash velouté around. Drizzle with a little olive oil and garnish with the sautéed cèpes and parmesan crisps. Serve at once.

Chilled tomato consommé with asparagus, peas, tomato concassé, and basil

THIS IS A LOVELY, LIGHT, REFRESHING SOUP TO MAKE WHEN RIPE, FLAVOURFUL TOMATOES ARE AVAILABLE. CLARIFYING THE STOCK TO GIVE A CRYSTAL CLEAR RESULT TAKES SOME TIME, BUT YOU CAN PREPARE THE CONSOMMÉ THE DAY BEFORE YOU INTEND TO SERVE IT.

[Illustrated on page 51]

Serves 4–6 as an appetizer

TOMATO CONSOMMÉ:
3 tbsp (45 mL) olive oil
1 onion, peeled and chopped
1 carrot, peeled and chopped
1 leek, trimmed and chopped
2 celery stalks, trimmed and chopped
1 bay leaf
Few thyme sprigs
1 tsp (5 mL) tomato paste
1½ lb (750 g) very ripe tomatoes, roughly chopped
2 garlic cloves, sliced
1 tsp (5 mL) granulated sugar
2 tsp (10 mL) sea salt
2 tsp (10 mL) chopped basil
2 tsp (10 mL) chopped tarragon
4 cups (1 L) tomato juice

FOR CLARIFYING:
7 oz (200 g) ripe tomatoes, roughly chopped
Handful of basil and tarragon stems, roughly chopped
¼ tsp (1 mL) white peppercorns
¼ tsp (1 mL) black peppercorns
6 egg whites

FOR SERVING:
Tomato concassé (see page 248)
Blanched asparagus spears, roughly chopped
Blanched green peas
Basil leaves, for garnish
Olive oil, for drizzling

TO MAKE THE TOMATO CONSOMMÉ, heat the olive oil in a large, heavy-based saucepan. Add the onion, carrot, leek, celery, bay leaf, and thyme and cook, stirring occasionally, until the vegetables are softened but not browned, about 10 minutes. Stir in the tomato paste, then add the chopped tomatoes. Cook for 10 minutes longer, stirring from time to time.

ADD THE GARLIC, SUGAR, SALT, chopped herbs, and tomato juice to the pan. Give the mixture a good stir and bring to a boil. Skim off any scum from the surface using a large spoon, then reduce the heat and let simmer gently for 15 minutes.

LINE A COLANDER with a large piece of cheesecloth and stand it over a large bowl. Pour the tomato liquid through the colander, pressing the vegetables with the back of a ladle to extract as much juice as possible. Discard the vegetable pulp. Set the bowl in a larger bowl half-filled with ice water to hasten cooling. Stir the tomato liquid frequently to encourage it to cool down quickly. Wash and sterilize the cheesecloth (you will need to use it again).

TO PREPARE THE CLARIFYING MIX, put the chopped tomatoes, basil and tarragon stems, peppercorns, and egg whites into a food processor and blend until the mixture is frothy.

POUR THE COLD TOMATO LIQUID into a large pan and add the clarifying mixture. Bring slowly to a boil, all the while whisking vigorously to create a layer of "egg white foam" over the surface. Once the liquid reaches a boil, reduce the heat and simmer gently, undisturbed, for 15 minutes; the stock will gradually become clear.

LINE THE COLANDER AGAIN with the clean cheesecloth and stand it over a large bowl. Carefully ladle the stock into the colander. If it is still cloudy, repeat the clarifying process with more whisked egg whites. Taste and adjust the seasoning, then chill the consommé for a few hours or overnight until required.

TO SERVE, put some tomato concassé, asparagus, and peas into each bowl or cappuccino cup, then pour in the tomato consommé. Garnish with a few basil leaves and add a drizzle of olive oil.

MAIN COURSES

Line-caught turbot roasted on the bone, with a garnish of stuffed baby peppers and spring vegetables

[Recipe on page 170]

Pan-roasted fillet of John Dory with crab, crushed new potatoes, and a basil vinaigrette

[Recipe on page 172]

Pan-grilled monkfish with confit duck, red and yellow peppers, and a red wine sauce

[Recipe on page 174]

Pan-roasted fillet of halibut with carrot and coriander pappardelle, baby turnips, salsify, and passion fruit sauce

[Recipe on page 176]

Halibut fillets larded with smoked salmon, served with candied lemon, braised vegetables, and smoked horseradish velouté

[Recipe on page 178]

Pan-fried sea bass with roasted baby artichokes, borlotti beans, and a cèpe velouté

[Recipe on page 180]

Roasted Bresse squab wrapped in prosciutto with foie gras, creamed mushrooms, and a date sauce

[Recipe on page 182]

Roasted duck breast with honey-glazed baby onions and salsify, minted peas, and a Madeira sauce

[Recipe on page 184]

Roasted saddle and leg of rabbit on cauliflower, haricot blanc, and baby lettuce, with a red wine sauce

[Recipe on page 186]

Roasted loin of venison with braised
red cabbage and parsnip chips

[Recipe on page 188]

Navarin of lamb with buttered
vegetables, celeriac purée,
and thyme jus

[Recipe on page 190]

Rack of lamb with confit shoulder,
Provençale vegetables,
spinach, and basil lamb jus

[Recipe on page 192]

Roasted filet of beef with a truffle
and root vegetable infusion

[Recipe on page 194]

Slow-braised pork belly with
langoustine, crushed peas, and
Madeira sauce

[Recipe on page 196]

Pork cheeks with pork filet wrapped
in prosciutto, black pudding, baby
turnips, and sautéed morels

[Recipe on page 198]

Veal osso bucco with boulangère
potatoes, Savoy cabbage, turnip
purée, and its own braising jus

[Recipe on page 200]

Risotto of cèpes with green onions,
grated truffle, and parmesan

[Recipe on page 202]

Line-caught turbot roasted on the bone, with a garnish of stuffed baby peppers and spring vegetables

I LOVE THE CLEAN FLAVOUR AND MEATY TEXTURE OF TURBOT. WE GET REALLY LARGE FISH, WHICH WE THEN CUT INTO CHUNKY STEAKS FOR ROASTING. FOR THIS RECIPE, YOU COULD COOK A SMALL WHOLE TURBOT: SIMPLY DRIZZLE IT WITH GARLIC OIL, SEASON WELL, AND ROAST FOR 20–25 MINUTES IN A HOT OVEN. *[Illustrated on page 54]*

Serves 2 as a main course

STUFFED BABY PEPPERS:
3–4 baby sweet peppers
3 tbsp (45 mL) olive oil, plus extra for drizzling
½ red sweet pepper, seeded and finely chopped
½ yellow sweet pepper, seeded and finely chopped
¼ small eggplant, trimmed and finely chopped
1 small zucchini, trimmed and finely chopped
Sea salt and black pepper

CITRUS SAUCE:
1 pink grapefruit
1 orange
1 lemon
Scant 1 cup (200 mL) Sauternes or other sweet dessert wine
Scant 1 cup (200 mL) fish stock (see page 246)
7 tbsp (105 mL) cold butter, diced
1–2 tsp (5–10 mL) granulated sugar (optional)

TURBOT:
1 turbot steak, about 12 oz (340 g)
2 tbsp (30 mL) olive oil
1 head of new season's garlic, halved lengthwise
1–2 tbsp (15–30 mL) butter, diced

SPRING VEGETABLES:
2 cups (500 mL) vegetable stock (see page 247) or water
1 head of baby cauliflower, cut into florets
8 oz (250 g) asparagus spears, trimmed
Olive oil, for drizzling
Scant 2 oz (50 g) snow peas
1 large carrot, peeled and cut into long strips with a mandoline

FIRST, PREPARE THE BABY PEPPERS. Use a blowtorch to scorch the skins until they are blackened and blistered all over. (Alternately, spear each one with a long-handled fork and turn over a gas flame until scorched.) Put the peppers into a bowl, cover with plastic wrap, and set aside while you cook the ratatouille stuffing (the steam trapped inside the bowl will help to lift the skin).

HEAT THE OLIVE OIL in a skillet and gently sauté the chopped peppers until softened, 2–3 minutes. Add the eggplant, zucchini, and some seasoning and cook until all the vegetables are tender, about 2–3 minutes longer. Tip into a large bowl and let cool.

PREHEAT THE OVEN to 200°F (100°C). Peel off the skin from the baby peppers, then put them into a small roasting pan and drizzle generously with olive oil. Roast for about 40–50 minutes to soften.

MAKE THE CITRUS SAUCE in the meantime. Peel and segment each fruit: Cut off the top and bottom, then cut away the skin and white pith, following the natural curve. Hold the fruit over a sieve set over a bowl to catch the juice and cut out the segments, using a small sharp knife. Squeeze the excess juice from the membrane, then discard.

PUT THE SAUTERNES IN A SAUCEPAN and boil to reduce by two-thirds. Add the stock and reduce again by two-thirds.

TIP IN THE CITRUS SEGMENTS and juice and bring back to a boil, whisking until the segments break apart. Lower the heat to a gentle simmer and whisk in the butter, a few pieces at a time. Taste and adjust the seasoning, adding salt, pepper, and a little sugar if the sauce is too acidic. If you prefer a smooth sauce, strain it through a fine sieve and discard the pulp.

WHEN THE PEPPERS ARE READY, cut off the tops and scoop out the seeds with a small spoon. Stuff with the ratatouille. Replace the tops and set in a small baking pan (ready to reheat for serving).

WHEN READY TO COOK, preheat the oven to 400°F (200°C). Season the turbot steak all over with salt and pepper. Heat a large stovetop-to-oven skillet or a sturdy roasting pan until hot, then add the olive oil and garlic, cut side down. When the garlic is golden, add the turbot steak and butter. Fry for 2 minutes on each side until golden brown, using the foaming butter to baste the fish. Transfer the skillet to the oven and roast until the fish is just slightly firm and cooked through, 6–8 minutes.

WHILE THE FISH IS COOKING, prepare the spring vegetables. Bring the stock to a boil in a pan. Blanch the cauliflower and asparagus in the stock for 2–3 minutes until tender. Remove with a slotted spoon, drizzle with a little olive oil and seasoning, and keep warm.

BLANCH THE SNOW PEAS and carrot strips for 1½ minutes, then drain well. Again, drizzle with a little olive oil and seasoning. Wrap the asparagus spears in the carrot ribbons, to make two bundles.

REMOVE THE FISH from the oven and let rest for a few minutes. Put the stuffed peppers in the oven to warm up. Gently reheat the citrus sauce.

TO SERVE, transfer the turbot steak and roasted garlic to a warm serving platter and arrange the cauliflower, snow peas, and carrot-wrapped asparagus spears alongside. Serve immediately, with the citrus sauce.

Pan-roasted fillet of John Dory with crab, crushed new potatoes, and a basil vinaigrette

JOHN DORY HAS A WONDERFUL, DELICATE FLAVOUR THAT MARRIES BEAUTIFULLY WITH WHITE CRABMEAT AND NEW POTATOES. DO NOT BE PUT OFF BY THE NUMBER OF DIFFERENT ELEMENTS IN THIS DISH. YOU CAN OMIT THE CAVIAR TORTELLINI, HERB CRISPS, AND GARLIC PURÉE IF YOU LIKE—THE DISH WILL STILL TASTE AMAZING. *[Illustrated on page 56]*

Serves 4 as a main course

JOHN DORY:

4 john dory fillets, skinned, about 5 oz (150 g) each
Sea salt and black pepper
2 tbsp (30 mL) olive oil
1 tbsp (15 mL) butter, diced

CAVIAR TORTELLINI:

Scant 2 oz (50 g) saffron pasta dough (see page 250)
8 scant tsp (scant 40 mL) caviar
1 egg white, beaten with 1 tsp (5 mL) water (egg wash)

TOMATO PETALS:

6–8 plum or roma tomatoes

CRUSHED POTATOES AND CRAB:

10 oz (300 g) boiling potatoes
4 tbsp (60 mL) classic vinaigrette (see page 249)
5 oz (150 g) white crabmeat
Small handful of chives, finely chopped
Few chervil sprigs, chopped

FOR SERVING:

Olive oil, for drizzling
Basil crisps (see page 248), optional
A little garlic purée (see page 250), optional
Basil vinaigrette (see page 249), for drizzling

CHECK THE JOHN DORY FILLETS for any pin bones, then cut each fillet in half. Wrap and refrigerate until ready to cook.

TO MAKE THE CAVIAR TORTELLINI, roll out the pasta as thinly as possible, using a pasta machine. It needs to be very fine: if necessary, roll it out further on a lightly floured surface using a rolling pin. Cut out 2–2½ inch (5–6 cm) rounds using a fluted pastry cutter and place a scant teaspoon (scant 5 mL) of caviar on one half of each round. Brush around the caviar with egg wash, then fold the pasta over the filling to form a semi-circle. Press the pasta edges together to seal. Now curl the semi-circle around your little finger and press the tips together to form tortellini shapes (illustrated on page 49). Keep refrigerated until ready to serve.

FOR THE TOMATO PETALS, put the tomatoes in a heatproof bowl, cover them with boiling water, and leave for 45–60 seconds to loosen the skins. Peel, quarter, and remove the seeds, then trim each to get four "tomato petals."

FOR THE CRUSHED POTATOES, cook the potatoes in well-salted boiling water until tender when pierced with a skewer, 10–12 minutes. Drain well. While still hot, peel off the skins with a small knife. Place in a bowl and lightly crush with a fork. Drizzle the vinaigrette over them, then add the crabmeat and mix with the fork to combine.

JUST BEFORE SERVING, season the john dory fillets and heat up a heavy-based skillet. When the pan is hot, add the olive oil, then the fish fillets, boned side down. Cook, without moving, until golden brown and cooked two-thirds through, 1½–2 minutes.

TURN THE FISH OVER and add the butter to the pan. Spoon the melted butter over the fish as it cooks. The fillets should only need a minute on the second side; they're ready when they feel slightly springy when pressed.

WARM UP THE CRUSHED NEW POTATOES. Fold through the chopped chives and chervil, then season with salt and pepper to taste.

BLANCH THE TORTELLINI in a pot of boiling salted water for 20 seconds only (you don't want the caviar to cook). Drain well and drizzle a little olive oil over them.

TO ASSEMBLE, press a layer of crushed new potatoes into a square on a warm plate (use a suitable mould if you have one). Arrange a layer of tomato petals on top, trimming them to fit neatly, then remove the mould. Arrange the john dory fillets on top. Sit two caviar tortellini on one side of the plate and drizzle on a little olive oil. Garnish the plate with a few basil crisps and dot with a little garlic purée, if you like. Spoon on the basil vinaigrette just before serving.

Pan-grilled monkfish with confit duck, red and yellow peppers, and a red wine sauce

WRAPPING MONKFISH IN DUCK CONFIT ENHANCES THE FLAVOUR AND KEEPS IT MOIST. WE ALSO CONFIT DUCK GIZZARDS TO USE AS A GARNISH, BUT I AM NOT SUGGESTING YOU DO SO. PREPARE THE CONFIT AND CHICKEN MOUSSE A DAY AHEAD, AND POACH THE MONKFISH A FEW HOURS IN ADVANCE, READY TO PAN-GRILL BEFORE SERVING. *[Illustrated on page 57]*

Serves 4 as a main course

CONFIT DUCK:
4 duck legs, about 6 oz (175 g) each
Sea salt and black pepper
Few thyme sprigs
1 bay leaf
1¼–1½ cups (300–350 mL) duck or goose fat, melted

CHICKEN MOUSSE:
1 skinless, boneless chicken breast half, about 4 oz (125 g), chopped
1 tbsp (15 mL) lemon juice
2 tbsp (30 mL) whipping cream

MONKFISH:
2 monkfish tail fillets, about 10 oz (300 g) each

PEPPERS:
1 red sweet pepper, quartered and seeded
1 yellow sweet pepper, quartered and seeded
3–4 tbsp (45–60 mL) tomato sauce (see page 249)

FOR SERVING:
Wilted baby leaf spinach
Garlic purée (see page 250), optional
Sautéed zucchini and shimeji mushrooms
Olive oil, for drizzling
½ quantity red wine sauce (see page 248)

FIRST, PREPARE THE CONFIT DUCK. Preheat the oven to 325°F (170°C). Season the duck legs with salt and pepper and place in a small roasting pan or Dutch oven in which they fit quite snugly. Add the thyme and bay leaf, then pour in enough duck fat to cover the legs. Lay a piece of crumpled parchment paper on top. Place over low heat and slowly bring the fat to a gentle simmer. Carefully transfer the pan to the oven and cook until the meat is meltingly tender and easily falls off the bone, 1½–2 hours. Cool the duck in the fat.

TO MAKE THE CHICKEN MOUSSE, put the chicken in a food processor with the lemon juice, cream, and some seasoning. Blitz to a smooth purée. To check the seasoning, blanch a little spoonful of the filling, then taste. Transfer the mousse to a bowl, cover with plastic wrap, and chill for 20 minutes to firm up slightly.

PAT THE MONKFISH TAILS DRY with paper towels, then season well. Spread half the chicken mousse on a large piece of plastic wrap to a rectangle, long and wide enough to wrap a monkfish tail. Lay a monkfish tail on the rectangle and wrap the chicken mousse around it, using the plastic wrap to help. Holding both ends of the wrap, roll the fish on the work surface to ensure that it is evenly covered with the mousse. Repeat with the other monkfish tail and remaining chicken mousse. Chill while you prepare the duck.

REMOVE THE DUCK LEGS from the fat and pat dry with paper towels. Strip the meat from the bones and finely shred with two forks. Put into a bowl and season well. Mix in a little duck fat to moisten. Divide the duck meat into two portions and place one on a large piece of plastic wrap. Spread out to a rectangle, large enough to envelop a monkfish roll. Unwrap one of the monkfish rolls and lay it on the duck meat. Wrap the meat around the roll, again using the wrap to help. (The chicken mousse will make the meat bind to the monkfish.) Grasp both ends of the wrap and roll the monkfish log to tighten and even out the shape. Repeat with the other monkfish roll and remaining confit duck. Secure the ends and chill for 1–2 hours until firm.

TO POACH THE MONKFISH, lower the rolls, still in the plastic wrap, into a pan of gently simmering water. Poach until just cooked through, 8–10 minutes. The fish should feel slightly springy when cooked. Cool completely and refrigerate if not serving immediately.

MEANWHILE, PREPARE THE PEPPERS. Preheat the broiler. Lay the peppers, skin side up, on a baking sheet and broil, close to the heat and turning occasionally, until the skins have blackened and blistered all over. Tip into a bowl, cover with plastic wrap, and set aside for a few minutes (the steam will help to lift the skin). Uncover and peel off the skins, then chop the peppers.

WHEN READY TO SERVE, preheat the oven to 400°F (200°C). Put the chopped peppers in a pan with the tomato sauce and warm through. Heat a ridged cast-iron grill pan until hot. Unwrap the monkfish rolls and pan-grill for about 2 minutes on each side until the confit duck coating is nicely charred. Transfer the fish to a rimmed baking sheet and place in the oven to heat for 4–5 minutes. Remove and let rest for a few minutes.

TO SERVE, spoon the peppers in tomato sauce into a rectangular metal mould set on a warm serving plate. Cover with a thin layer of spinach, then remove the mould. Repeat for the remaining plates. Thinly slice the monkfish and arrange on the spinach. Dot a little garlic purée around the plate, if you like. Garnish with sautéed zucchini and mushrooms, drizzle a little olive oil over, and spoon on the red wine sauce.

Pan-roasted fillet of halibut with carrot and coriander pappardelle, baby turnips, salsify, and passion fruit sauce

THIS PRESENTATION REALLY SHOWCASES HALIBUT STEAKS, BUT YOU CAN SIMPLIFY THE DISH AT HOME. SERVE THE FISH ON A POOL OF PASSION FRUIT SAUCE, SURROUNDED BY THE SAUTÉED VEGETABLES, WITH A BOWL OF CORIANDER PAPPARDELLE OR GLAZED BABY CARROTS ON THE SIDE. *[Illustrated on page 60]*

Serves 4 as a main course

CORIANDER PAPPARDELLE:

8 oz (250 g) Italian "00" pasta flour (about 2 cups/500 mL), sifted

1/4 tsp (1 mL) fine sea salt

Small bunch of coriander (about 1 oz/30 g), leaves finely chopped

2 extra large eggs, plus 3 extra large egg yolks

1 tbsp (15 mL) olive oil

CARROT PAPPARDELLE:

2 very large carrots, peeled

Olive oil, for drizzling

PASSION FRUIT SAUCE:

2 large passion fruit, halved

7 tbsp (105 mL) sweet dessert wine (such as Montbazillac)

1/3 cup (75 mL) whipping cream

1–2 tbsp (15–30 mL) cold butter, diced

SAUTÉED TURNIPS, SALSIFY, AND MUSHROOMS:

Scant 4 oz (100 g) baby turnips, trimmed and quartered

Scant 4 oz (100 g) salsify, trimmed

Juice of 1/2 lemon

1 tbsp (15 mL) olive oil

2 tbsp (30 mL) butter

Scant 4 oz (100 g) shimeji mushrooms, trimmed

2 tsp (10 mL) chopped flat-leaf parsley

1 tsp (5mL) chopped coriander leaves

HALIBUT:

4 halibut fillets, skinned, about 5 oz (150 g) each

2 tbsp (30 mL) olive oil

1 tbsp (15 mL) butter, diced

1 tbsp (15 mL) each chopped flat-leaf parsley and coriander

FOR SERVING:

Wilted baby romaine lettuce

8 blanched asparagus spears

Turnip purée (see page 250), optional

Basil crisps (see page 248), optional

FOR THE CORIANDER PAPPARDELLE, put the flour, salt, and chopped coriander into a food processor. Beat together the eggs, egg yolks, and olive oil. Add three-quarters of this to the processor and blitz to fine crumbs, stopping to scrape down the sides a few times. If the dough seems too dry and doesn't come together when pressed with your fingers, add a little more egg and blitz again. Tip the dough onto a lightly floured board and knead for a few minutes until smooth and slightly springy. Wrap in plastic wrap and rest for at least 30 minutes before using.

ROLL OUT THE PASTA THINLY, using a pasta machine, to sheets $\frac{1}{16}$ inch (2 mm) thick. Lightly flour the pasta sheets and cut into strips $1\frac{1}{2}$ inches (4 cm) wide. Set aside on a baking sheet, separating the layers of pasta with waxed paper or parchment paper.

FOR THE CARROT PAPPARDELLE, peel the carrots and slice into long strips, using a mandoline. Blanch in boiling salted water for 1 minute, then refresh in ice water. Drain well and lay the strips flat on a baking sheet. Cover with plastic wrap and refrigerate until ready to use.

TO MAKE THE PASSION FRUIT SAUCE, scrape out the passion fruit seeds and juice from the fruit into a saucepan and add the dessert wine. Boil until reduced by half, then add the cream. Simmer until reduced to the consistency of a thick but pourable cream. Strain through a fine sieve into a clean saucepan and season well to taste. Set aside.

ADD THE TURNIPS to a pot of boiling salted water and blanch for 2 minutes, then drain and set aside. Peel the salsify, cut into $1\frac{1}{4}$-inch (3-cm) lengths, and immediately blanch in boiling water with the lemon juice added for 2 minutes. Drain and set aside with the turnips.

WHEN READY TO COOK, heat a skillet, then add the olive oil and butter. Tip in the baby turnips, salsify, and mushrooms and sauté over high heat for a few minutes until the mushrooms are cooked. Add the chopped herbs and take the pan off the heat. Keep warm.

ADD THE CORIANDER PAPPARDELLE to a pot of boiling salted water. Blanch for 1 minute, then add the carrot strips and cook for 30–60 seconds longer. Drain well, then dress with a little olive oil and keep warm.

SEASON THE HALIBUT FILLETS with salt and pepper. Heat the olive oil in a heavy-based skillet and fry them, without moving, until golden brown on the base, $1\frac{1}{2}$–2 minutes. Turn the fillets over and add the butter and chopped herbs. Cook for 1–$1\frac{1}{2}$ minutes longer, spooning the melted butter over the fish to baste it as it cooks. The fillets are ready when they feel slightly springy when pressed.

TO FINISH THE SAUCE, whisk in the cold butter over low heat.

TO SERVE, put a layer of wilted lettuce on each warm serving plate. Twirl a coriander pappardelle and a carrot pappardelle around a carving fork, then slide on top of the lettuce. Sit a halibut fillet on top, then finish with a pair of blanched asparagus spears. Drain off the excess oil from the sautéed vegetables and arrange around the plate, with little dollops of turnip purée, if using. Garnish with some basil crisps, if you like. Spoon on the passion fruit sauce and serve.

Halibut fillets larded with smoked salmon, with candied lemon, braised vegetables, and smoked horseradish velouté THIS

DELICATE FISH DISH HAS A LOVELY SUMMERY FEEL. SLIVERS OF SMOKED SALMON THREADED THROUGH THE HALIBUT ADD ANOTHER DIMENSION, AND WAFER-THIN CANDIED LEMON SLICES LEND A ZESTY FINISH. YOU WILL FIND IT EASIER TO HANDLE THE SMOKED SALMON IF YOU PARTIALLY FREEZE IT FIRST.

[Illustrated on page 63]

Serves 4 as a main course

CANDIED LEMON SLICES:
1 large lemon, scrubbed
1-/4 cups (300 mL) stock syrup (see page 251)

HALIBUT:
4 halibut fillets, skinned, about 5 oz (150 g) each
5 oz (150 g) smoked salmon, in one piece, partially frozen
2 tbsp (30 mL) olive oil
1 tbsp (15 mL) butter, diced
Splash of fish stock (see page 246) or water
Few chives, finely chopped
Few chervil sprigs, finely chopped
Few flat-leaf parsley sprigs, finely chopped

SMOKED HORSERADISH VELOUTÉ:
2 shallots, peeled and finely chopped
2 tbsp (30 mL) olive oil
Sea salt and black pepper
1/4 cup (50 mL) dry white wine
1/4 cup (50 mL) fish stock (see page 246)
2/3 cup (150 mL) whipping cream
2 tbsp (30 mL) smoked horseradish cream
2 tsp (10 mL) lemon juice, or to taste

BRAISED VEGETABLES:
Scant 4 oz (100 g) baby leeks, trimmed
1 baby fennel bulb, trimmed
5 oz (150 g) artichoke hearts, trimmed
Scant 4 oz (100 g) radishes, trimmed
4 tsp (20 mL) butter
Scant 1 cup (200 mL) vegetable stock (see page 247)
Herb sprigs (such as chervil, chives, and dillweed), for garnish

BRAISED LETTUCE HEARTS:
2 tbsp (30 mL) olive oil
2 small heads of romaine lettuce, trimmed
1–2 tbsp (15–30 mL) butter
Splash of vegetable stock or water

FIRST, PREPARE THE CANDIED LEMON SLICES: Cut off the ends of the lemon, then slice it as thinly as possible, using a sharp knife or a mandoline. Meanwhile, boil the stock syrup in a small saucepan for 2 minutes. Drop in the lemon slices and simmer them for 3–4 minutes, then take the pan off the heat. Let the lemons steep in the syrup overnight. (If not using immediately, transfer to a clean jar, cover, and keep in the fridge for up to a month.)

TO PREPARE THE FISH, trim the halibut fillets to neaten, and remove any pin bones. Cut the smoked salmon into 8 long, thin strips, ¼ inch (5 mm) in diameter. Use a larding needle to grip one end of a salmon strip and pull it through a halibut fillet from one side to the other, about one-third of the way along the fillet. Thread another strip through, two-thirds of the way along the fillet. Lard each of the remaining halibut fillets with two smoked salmon strips in the same way. (If you do not have a larding needle, use a fish knife to cut one or two slits through each fillet, then stuff the "pockets" with frozen strips of smoked salmon.) Trim the smoked salmon strips, if necessary. Wrap the fish in plastic wrap and refrigerate.

FOR THE SMOKED HORSERADISH VELOUTÉ, sweat the shallots with the olive oil and a little seasoning in a heavy-based saucepan until soft but not brown, 4–6 minutes.

DEGLAZE THE PAN with the wine and let bubble until it has almost totally evaporated. Add the fish stock, bring to a boil, and reduce by half. Add the cream and smoked horseradish and let bubble until the consistency of a thick but still pourable cream. Strain the sauce through a fine sieve into a clean pan. Taste for seasoning, adding salt, pepper, and a little lemon juice to taste. Set aside until ready to serve.

WHEN READY TO SERVE, prepare the braised vegetables. Cut the leeks into 1¼-inch (3-cm) lengths; thinly slice the fennel; quarter the artichoke hearts and radishes. Melt the butter in a pan over medium heat. Add the leeks, fennel, artichoke hearts, and some seasoning. Cook for 2 minutes, then add the radishes. Pour in the vegetable stock and bring to a simmer, then cover and braise until tender, about 4 minutes.

MEANWHILE, COOK THE FISH. Heat the 2 tbsp (30 mL) olive oil in a large skillet until you can feel the heat rising. Season the halibut fillets and fry, without moving, until golden brown on the base, 2–3 minutes. Add the butter and turn the fillets over. Splash in a little fish stock and cook for 30–60 seconds longer, basting the fish with the pan juices. The fillets should feel slightly springy when pressed. Throw in the chopped herbs and spoon the sauce over the fish to coat. Remove from the pan and let rest while you wilt the lettuce.

HEAT A LITTLE OLIVE OIL in a large skillet over high heat. Quarter the lettuce hearts and place, cut side down, in the pan with a few pieces of butter. Add a splash of stock and braise the lettuce until wilted, 2–3 minutes. Season well, and drain off the excess liquid.

IN THE MEANTIME, gently reheat the smoked horseradish velouté.

TO SERVE, divide the braised lettuce among warm serving plates and place the halibut fillets on top. Arrange the braised vegetables around the plates and garnish with little sprigs of herbs. Place a slice of candied lemon on top of each halibut fillet. Pass the smoked horseradish velouté around separately.

Pan-fried sea bass with roasted baby artichokes, borlotti beans, and a cèpe velouté

SEA BASS FILLETS ARE MATCHED WITH ROASTED BABY ARTICHOKES AND BORLOTTI BEANS FOR A SIMPLE FISH DISH THAT TASTES DIVINE. COOK THE BEANS AND MAKE THE BEAN PURÉE WELL IN ADVANCE. TO MAKE LIFE EASIER, SERVE WITH A SIMPLE NEST OF PAPPARDELLE, RATHER THAN TIGHT CURLS ARRANGED AROUND THE PLATE. *[Illustrated on page 64]*

Serves 4 as a main course

BRAISED BORLOTTI BEANS:
¾ cup (175 mL) dried borlotti beans (cranberry beans), soaked overnight in cold water
1 small carrot, peeled
1 onion, peeled
1 celery stalk, halved
2½-oz (75-g) piece of pancetta skin
1 bay leaf
2½ cups (600 mL) chicken stock (see page 246)
Sea salt and black pepper

CÈPE VELOUTÉ:
½ oz (15 g) dried cèpes (or porcini)
2 tbsp (30 mL) olive oil
1 large shallot, peeled and finely chopped
1 cup (250 mL) Noilly Prat (or other dry vermouth)
2 cups (500 mL) chicken stock (see page 246)
1 cup (250 mL) whipping cream

ROASTED BABY VIOLET ARTICHOKES:
Scant 4 oz (100 g) baby violet artichokes
1 lemon, halved
1–2 tbsp (15–30 mL) butter
¼ cup (50 mL) dry white wine
¼ cup (50 mL) chicken stock (see page 246)

SEA BASS:
4 sea bass fillets, about 5 oz (150 g) each, with skin
2 tbsp (30 mL) olive oil

FOR SERVING:
Wilted baby romaine lettuce
Scant 4 oz (100 g) fresh pappardelle, blanched and curled into rolls (optional)
Olive oil, for drizzling

FIRST, COOK THE BORLOTTI BEANS. Drain the beans and place in a saucepan with the flavouring vegetables, pancetta skin, bay leaf, chicken stock, and some pepper. Bring to a boil and boil steadily for 10 minutes, then lower the heat and simmer the beans until they are soft, 1½–2 hours. Add salt toward the end of the cooking time.

FOR THE CÈPE VELOUTÉ, put the dried cèpes in a small bowl, pour on enough boiling water to cover, and let soak. Meanwhile, heat the olive oil in a heavy-based pan and sweat the shallot with a little seasoning, stirring occasionally, until soft, 6–8 minutes. Deglaze the pan with the vermouth and let bubble until the pan is almost dry. Remove the cèpes from their liquid and add to the pan with three-quarters of the soaking liquid (leaving the sediment in the bowl). Pour in the chicken stock, bring to a boil, and boil vigorously until reduced by half. Add the cream and return to a boil. Reduce again until the consistency of a thick but still pourable cream. Strain the velouté through a fine sieve into a clean saucepan. Taste and adjust the seasoning.

PREPARE THE ARTICHOKES one at a time: Squeeze the juice from ½ lemon into a bowl of ice water. Cut off the tip, then cut away the tough outer leaves from the artichoke with a small sharp knife, until you reach the tender, pale green leaves. Trim off the tough skin from the stalk and base, then drop the artichoke into the water.

WHEN THE BEANS ARE COOKED, remove the vegetables, bay leaf, and pancetta skin, leaving the beans and liquid in the pan. Use a slotted spoon to transfer half of the beans to a food processor. Add a little of the hot liquid and blend to a smooth purée, stopping to scrape down the sides once or twice. Add a little more liquid if the purée seems too thick, and season with salt and pepper to taste. Set the purée and whole beans aside until ready to serve.

DRAIN THE ARTICHOKES, cut them in half, and rub the cut sides with lemon. Melt the butter in a skillet and fry the artichoke halves, cut side down, until golden brown and lightly caramelized, 2–3 minutes. Turn them over. Deglaze the pan with the wine and let bubble until almost all evaporated before adding the stock. Lower the heat slightly and let the artichokes simmer until tender when pierced, 10–15 minutes.

WHEN READY TO SERVE, gently reheat the borlotti beans and bean purée.

TRIM, LIGHTLY SCORE, AND SEASON the sea bass fillets. Heat a large skillet until hot and add the olive oil. Place the fish in the pan, skin side down, and fry until the skin is golden brown and crisp, and the fish is cooked two-thirds of the way through, 2½–3 minutes. Turn the fillets over and cook on the flesh side for 30–60 seconds. When cooked, the thickest part of the fillets should feel slightly springy when pressed.

TO SERVE, spoon a bed of wilted lettuce onto each warm plate, using a round metal cutter to create a neat presentation. Remove the cutter and place the sea bass fillets, skin side up, on top of the lettuce. Squeeze little dots of bean purée around the plate, then arrange whole borlotti beans, artichoke halves, and pappardelle rolls, if using, in a ring. Drizzle the plate with a little olive oil and pour on a little cèpe velouté as you serve.

Roasted Bresse squab wrapped in prosciutto with foie gras, creamed mushrooms, and a date sauce

AN ELEGANT MAIN DISH, FEATURING FRESH CÈPES, CONFIT SQUAB LEGS, AND JUICY SQUAB BREASTS. COOK THE CONFIT, MAKE THE SAUCES, AND PREPARE THE SQUAB BREAST PACKAGES READY FOR COOKING A DAY IN ADVANCE, AND YOU WILL FIND THIS AN EASY DISH TO ASSEMBLE AND SERVE AT THE LAST MINUTE. *[Illustrated on page 69]*

Serves 4 as a main course

SQUAB:
4 squab pigeons (preferably Bresse)
8 oz (250 g) foie gras, deveined (see page 151)
Few thyme sprigs
1 bay leaf
½ tsp (2 mL) rock salt
Sea salt and black pepper
1¼ cups (300 mL) goose or duck fat, melted
4 slices of prosciutto (preferably prosciutto di Parma)
2 tbsp (30 mL) olive oil
1 tbsp (15 mL) butter, diced

DATE SAUCE:
4 oz (125 g) pitted dates, chopped
2 tbsp (30 mL) chilled butter, diced
1 quantity red wine sauce (see page 248)

CREAMED MUSHROOMS:
4 tsp (20 mL) butter
7 oz (200 g) fresh cèpes (porcini), cleaned and chopped
4 tbsp (60 mL) whipping cream

TO PREPARE THE SQUAB, remove the legs and set aside for the confit. Take the breasts off the bone, wrap in plastic wrap, and keep refrigerated until ready to use. Cut the foie gras into 4 even pieces and wrap in plastic wrap. To get nicely squared sides, if required, press each piece against the side of a square cake pan. Freeze for 1–2 hours until the foie gras pieces are solid.

TO CONFIT THE SQUAB LEGS, put them into a small saucepan with the thyme, bay leaf, rock salt, and ½ tsp (2 mL) black pepper. Cover with the melted goose fat, then put a small piece of wet parchment paper on top. Heat the fat to a slow simmer and let the legs cook very gently until the meat is tender, about 1 hour. Remove from the heat.

TAKE THE FOIE GRAS from the freezer, unwrap, and season lightly with salt and pepper. Heat a skillet until very hot, then sear the foie gras pieces for a few seconds on each side until lightly coloured; you don't want them to cook through. Remove from the pan and let cool, then wrap and freeze again until firm.

FOR THE DATE SAUCE, put the dates in a small saucepan and add just enough water to cover. Bring to a boil and cook until soft and pulpy, 10–12 minutes. While still hot, transfer to a small food processor and blend to a fine purée.

RETURN THE DATE PURÉE to the pan and place over low heat. Add a little of the red wine sauce to loosen the purée, then whisk in the butter a few pieces at a time. Season with salt and pepper to taste. Cool slightly, then pour the sauce into a squeezy bottle.

WHEN FIRM, remove the foie gras from the freezer. Lay the prosciutto slices out on a board. Unwrap the foie gras and season the squab breasts. Sandwich each piece of foie gras between two squab breasts, using the smaller filets on the side to cover any gaps between the breasts. Place each sandwich at the end of a prosciutto slice and roll up. Wrap in plastic wrap and refrigerate.

WHEN READY TO COOK, preheat the oven to 400°F (200°C). Heat a stovetop-to-oven sauté pan and add the olive oil. Unwrap the squab breast packages and place in the pan. Sear for 1½ minutes on each side until the prosciutto is browned all over, then transfer the pan to the oven. Roast until the squab breasts are medium rare, 5–7 minutes; they should feel slightly springy when pressed. Let rest in a warm place for a few minutes.

TO COOK THE MUSHROOMS, melt the butter in a sauté pan until it begins to foam. Add the mushrooms with some seasoning and sauté until golden brown, 3–4 minutes. Stir in the cream and take the pan off the heat. In another pan, warm up the remaining red wine sauce.

HEAT A SKILLET UNTIL HOT. Remove the squab legs from the fat and add to the skillet with a little seasoning, the butter, and a splash of red wine sauce. Cook the squab legs, basting with the melted butter and sauce, until nicely glazed, 2–3 minutes. Remove the pan from the heat.

TO SERVE, squeeze parallel lines of date sauce onto each warm plate. Arrange a pile of creamed mushrooms on one side, using a round metal cutter for a neat presentation. Top with the squab legs. Trim the ends of the squab breast packages, then cut in half. Arrange these on the plates and serve immediately, with the rest of the red wine sauce passed around separately.

Roasted duck breast with honey-glazed baby onions and salsify, minted peas, and a Madeira sauce

SWEET NEW SEASON PEAS, GLAZED BABY ONIONS, AND SALSIFY ARE THE PERFECT ACCOMPANIMENTS FOR SUCCULENT DUCK BREASTS. WHEN FRESH MORELS ARE IN SEASON, THEIR UNIQUE FLAVOUR ADDS A FURTHER DIMENSION; OTHERWISE YOU CAN SERVE SAUTÉED CÈPES OR CREMINO MUSHROOMS, IF YOU LIKE. *[Illustrated on page 70]*

Serves 4 as a main course

GLAZED ONIONS AND SALSIFY:
Scant 4 oz (100 g) baby onions
2 medium salsify
Juice of ½ lemon, or to taste
1 tsp (5 mL) olive oil
4 tsp (20 mL) butter
1½ tbsp (25 mL) clear honey

CRUSHED PEAS:
2 cups (500 mL) shelled fresh green peas
Small bunch of mint, leaves only
Olive oil, for drizzling

DUCK BREASTS:
4 duck breast halves, skin lightly scored
Sea salt and black pepper

FOR SERVING:
1 quantity Madeira sauce (see page 248)
Wilted spinach
Sautéed morels
Celeriac purée (see page 250), optional
Olive oil, for drizzling

TO PREPARE THE ONIONS, immerse them in boiling water for 1 minute to loosen the skins, then drain and peel. Add the onions to a fresh pan of boiling water and simmer until tender when pierced with a skewer, 15–20 minutes. Drain well and pat dry with paper towels. Set aside.

PEEL AND TRIM THE SALSIFY, then cut into batons 1–1¼ inches (2–3 cm) long. Immediately immerse in a pan of cold water with a generous squeeze of lemon juice added (the lemon juice helps to prevent discoloration). Bring the water to a boil, then remove from the heat and let the salsify cool in the pan.

FOR THE CRUSHED PEAS, add the peas and mint to a pan of boiling water and blanch for 2–3 minutes, then drain and tip into a food processor. Add a generous drizzle of olive oil and pulse for a few seconds until lightly crushed, but not puréed. Transfer to a bowl and season with salt and pepper to taste. Set aside.

WHEN READY TO COOK, preheat the oven to 425°F (220°C). Heat a large stovetop-to-oven skillet until hot. Season the duck breasts and place, skin side down, in the pan. Cook until the skin is golden brown, 3–4 minutes, then turn and sear briefly on the other side. Transfer the pan to the oven. Cook for 6–8 minutes, then remove and let rest in a warm place for 3–4 minutes.

TO GLAZE THE ONIONS AND SALSIFY, heat the olive oil in a sauté pan. Drain the salsify and pat dry. Add to the hot pan with the onions and fry over high heat until they start to colour. Add the butter, honey, a squeeze of lemon juice, and some seasoning. Toss for a few minutes until nicely caramelized. Taste and adjust the seasoning.

WHEN READY TO SERVE, warm up the Madeira sauce and crushed peas. Place a round metal cutter on a warm serving plate, spoon in a layer of crushed peas, and level with the back of a spoon. Top with a thin layer of warm spinach, then remove the cutter. Repeat with the other plates. Slice the duck breasts and arrange, overlapping, on the spinach. Alternate the morels, baby onions, and salsify in a ring around the plates, adding little spoonfuls of celeriac purée, if using. Drizzle on a little olive oil, and spoon the Madeira sauce over the duck.

Roasted saddle and leg of rabbit on cauliflower, haricot blanc, and baby lettuce, with a red wine sauce
WE ACCOMPANY THIS RABBIT DISH WITH WHOLEGRAIN MUSTARD—SERVED ON EDIBLE SPOONS MADE FROM GRISSINI DOUGH SPECKLED WITH POPPY SEEDS, BUT A POT OF GRAINY MUSTARD ON THE TABLE WILL DO! PREPARE THE STUFFED SADDLE OF RABBIT, READY FOR ROASTING, A DAY AHEAD. *[Illustrated on page 71]*

Serves 2–3 as a main course

RABBIT:
1 rabbit, about 3 lb (1.5 kg)
1 bay leaf
Few thyme sprigs
½ tsp (2 mL) black peppercorns
1 tsp (5 mL) coarse sea salt
1 lb (500 g) goose or duck fat, melted (approx)
Small handful of chives, finely chopped
Sea salt and black pepper
2–3 tbsp (30–45 mL) olive oil
Scant 2 oz (50 g) trompette de la mort (or other fresh wild mushrooms), roughly chopped
Scant 3 oz (85 g) caul fat or crepinette

SAUTÉED CAULIFLOWER, HARICOT BLANC, AND BABY LETTUCE:
1 head of baby cauliflower, cut into small florets
Few baby romaine lettuce leaves
2–3 artichoke hearts, chopped
2 tbsp (30 mL) olive oil
¼ cup (50 mL) cooked haricot blanc (e.g. cannellini or navy beans)
1–2 tbsp (15–30 mL) butter, diced

FOR SERVING:
Olive oil, for drizzling
1 quantity red wine sauce (see page 248)

TO CUT UP THE RABBIT, first carve out the legs. To do so, cut through until you reach the leg joint. Snap the joint back, then cut the leg off. Repeat with the other legs. With a strong knife, chop off the end of the carcass inside the pelvic bone. Chop off the lower ribs, in between the saddle and rib cage, to get two small connecting racks (with two rib bones per rack). Cut the racks in two, then use a small sharp knife to cut ¾ inch (2 cm) of meat away at the thin end of the rack to expose the bones and get a French trim. Slide the knife under the saddle and cut it away from the bone. Wrap and refrigerate the pieces of meat (but not the legs) until ready to assemble.

FOR THE CONFIT RABBIT, preheat the oven to 325°F (170°C). Put the rabbit legs in a Dutch oven with the bay leaf, thyme, peppercorns, and coarse salt, then pour in the melted goose fat, making sure the legs are completely submerged. Cover with a piece of wet parchment paper that fits snugly, to keep the meat submerged during cooking. Put into the oven and cook until the meat is very tender, about 1½ hours.

LET THE RABBIT LEGS COOL in the fat, then them take out and scrape off the excess fat, herbs, and peppercorns. Strip the meat from the bones and remove any fat or sinew. Shred the meat, place in a large bowl, and moisten with a little of the confit fat. Stir in the chopped chives and season with salt and pepper to taste.

PUT TWO LAYERS of plastic wrap on a work surface. Spoon the confit rabbit on top and press to form a tight log, 1–1¼ inches (2–3 cm) in diameter, using the plastic wrap to help shape it. Wrap and roll the log to even out the thickness. Chill for a few hours until firm.

TO PREPARE THE STUFFED SADDLE, heat 1 tbsp (15 mL) olive oil in a pan over high heat. Add the mushrooms and season, then toss over a high heat for 3–4 minutes to soften. Tip onto a plate and let cool.

MEANWHILE, separate the two filets from the rabbit saddle. Without cutting right through, cut a slit along the length of each filet (so it can open out like a book). Season both sides of the filets and open them out on top of the caul fat. Spoon the sautéed mushrooms along the length of the filets. Unwrap the confit, cut a piece to fit the length of each filet, and place on top of the mushrooms. Fold over one side of each filet to enclose the confit and mushrooms. Wrap each filet in a double layer of caul fat. Wrap each log tightly in plastic wrap. Grip both ends and roll on the surface to even out the shape. Chill for 1–2 hours until firm.

BRING A POT OF WATER to a gentle simmer. Lower the stuffed rabbit filets (still in the plastic wrap) into the water and poach until they are cooked through, 12–15 minutes; they should feel firm when pressed. Let cool completely.

WHEN READY TO COOK, heat the oven to 400°F (200°C). Blanch the cauliflower in boiling salted water for 1 minute, then refresh in cold water and drain. Shred the lettuce leaves and put to one side with the cauliflower and artichoke hearts.

HEAT A HEAVY ROASTING PAN or a large stovetop-to-oven skillet until hot, then add a little olive oil. Unwrap the stuffed rabbit filets and fry, turning, until lightly golden all over, 3–4 minutes. Transfer the pan to the oven and roast for 5–6 minutes to heat through.

MEANWHILE, fry the rabbit racks in a little oil over high heat until golden brown, 2–3 minutes. Transfer to the roasting pan in the oven and roast for 3–4 minutes or until done to your taste. Let the filets and racks rest in a warm place for a few minutes while you warm up the sauce and sauté the vegetables.

HEAT THE OLIVE OIL in a large sauté pan and sauté the cauliflower, haricot blanc, and artichoke hearts over high heat for a few minutes until light golden and hot. Stir in the lettuce and butter.

TO SERVE, place the sautéed vegetables and beans in two neat piles on each warm plate. Cut each stuffed rabbit filet into thick slices and place on top of the vegetables. Cut the racks into individual chops and arrange on the plates. Add a drizzle of olive oil and spoon the red wine sauce over the top.

Roasted loin of venison with braised red cabbage and parsnip chips

THIS DISH REALLY CAPTURES THE TASTES OF AUTUMN—FULL-FLAVOURED GAME, RED CABBAGE, ROOT VEGETABLES, AND FRESH CÈPES. THERE ARE SEVERAL DIFFERENT ELEMENTS HERE, BUT YOU CAN PREPARE THE BRAISED CABBAGE, PARSNIP PURÉE, AND BEET FONDANT AHEAD, READY TO REHEAT BEFORE SERVING. OMIT THE PARSNIP CHIPS, IF YOU LIKE. *[Illustrated on page 74]*

Serves 4 as a main course

BRAISED RED CABBAGE:
1 small head of red cabbage, trimmed
7 tbsp (105 mL) butter
¾ cup (175 mL) packed light brown sugar
⅓ cup (75 mL) sherry or red wine vinegar

PARSNIP PURÉE:
2 parsnips
⅔ cup (150 mL) milk
⅓ cup (75 mL) whipping cream
2 tbsp (30 mL) butter
Sea salt and black pepper

BEET FONDANT:
2 beets
2 tbsp (30 mL) butter
1 tsp (5 mL) olive oil
½ cup (125 mL) vegetable stock (see page 247) or chicken stock (see page 246)

PARSNIP CHIPS:
2 medium parsnips
Peanut oil, for deep-frying

VENISON:
1 venison filet (tenderloin), about 1¼ lb (625 g)
1½ tbsp (25 mL) olive oil
1–2 tbsp (15–30 mL) butter, diced

CREAMED CÈPES:
4 tsp (20 mL) butter
7 oz (200 g) fresh cèpes (porcini), cleaned and chopped
4 tbsp (60 mL) whipping cream

FOR SERVING:
1 quantity red wine sauce (see page 248)
Olive oil, for drizzling

FIRST, PREPARE THE RED CABBAGE. Halve, core, and finely shred the cabbage. Melt the butter with the sugar and vinegar in a pan. When the sugar has dissolved, tip in the cabbage and toss to coat. Cover with a crumpled piece of parchment paper and cook over low heat until the cabbage is tender, about 1½ hours. (Lift the paper and stir the cabbage every now and then.) At the end of cooking, if there is still a fair amount of liquid, drain the cabbage and set aside while you boil the liquid to reduce to a syrupy sauce, then pour it over the cabbage and toss to coat.

NEXT, PREPARE THE PARSNIP PURÉE. Peel the parsnips and finely slice the thinner ends. Cut the thicker ends into quarters and cut out the tough cores, then thinly slice. Put into a saucepan with the milk and cook until very soft, 20–25 minutes. Tip the cooked parsnips into a blender with about half of the milk and blend to a fine purée, adding a little more of the milk, if necessary. Return to the pan and stir in the cream and butter. Season with salt and pepper to taste. Transfer to a squeezy bottle and keep warm in a pan of hot water.

FOR THE BEET FONDANT, peel the beets and cut into rounds about ⅝ inch (1.5 cm) thick. Heat 1 tbsp (15 mL) butter and the olive oil in a sauté pan. Season the beet rounds and fry for about 2 minutes on each side until browned. Pour in the stock and bring to a boil.

DOT THE BEETROOT with the rest of the butter, in small pieces, then put a piece of parchment paper on top. Lower the heat and simmer gently until most of the stock has been absorbed and the beets are tender, 10–15 minutes.

TO MAKE THE PARSNIP CHIPS, peel the parsnips and finely slice into long ribbons, using a mandoline or a swivel peeler. Heat the peanut oil in a deep saucepan or deep-fryer until hot. (A piece of bread dropped in should sizzle immediately.) Fry the parsnips in batches until golden brown all over and crisp. Drain on paper towels and sprinkle with a little sea salt. Keep warm in a low oven.

WHEN READY TO SERVE, preheat the oven to 400°F (200°C). Season the venison with salt and pepper. Heat a stovetop-to-oven skillet, then add the olive oil. When hot, add the venison and brown it for 4–5 minutes, turning to colour evenly and adding the butter after a minute or so; as it melts and foams, spoon it over the venison to baste. Transfer the skillet to the oven and roast the venison until it is medium rare, 6–8 minutes; it should feel lightly springy when pressed. Remove and let rest in a warm place for a few minutes.

MEANWHILE, COOK THE CÈPES. Melt the butter in a sauté pan until it begins to foam. Add the cèpes, season, and sauté until golden brown, 3–4 minutes. Stir in the cream and remove from the heat. Warm up the red wine sauce.

TO SERVE, put a neat pile of braised red cabbage in the centre of each warm plate and top with the beet fondant and a generous spoonful of creamed cèpes. Squeeze little dots of parsnip purée around the plates. Slice the venison thickly and arrange, overlapping, over the creamed cèpes. Carefully pour the red wine sauce around the plates and drizzle with a little olive oil. Garnish with the parsnip chips.

Navarin of lamb with buttered vegetables, celeriac purée, and thyme jus

THIS IS THE PERFECT DISH TO SERVE IN THE SPRING WHEN NEW SEASON LAMB AND BABY VEGETABLES ARE AROUND. THE RECIPE MAKES MORE CONFIT THAN YOU WILL NEED HERE, BUT YOU CAN FREEZE WHAT IS LEFT OVER TO USE FOR THE LAMB RECIPE ON THE NEXT PAGE, OR AS A FILLING FOR RAVIOLI OR TORTELLINI. *[Illustrated on page 75]*

Serves 4 as a main course

CONFIT OF LAMB SHOULDER:
1 boned shoulder of lamb, about 2¼ lb (1 kg), skinned
1 tsp (5 mL) rock salt
Few thyme sprigs, plus 1 tbsp (15 mL) leaves
Few rosemary sprigs
1 bay leaf
½ head of garlic, cloves separated (unpeeled)
6–8 cups (1.5–2 L) duck or goose fat, melted
Sea salt and black pepper
1 tbsp (15 mL) olive oil

LAMB LOIN:
1 loin of lamb, about 1¼ lb (625 g), trimmed
1½ tbsp (25 mL) olive oil

THYME JUS:
1 quantity lamb jus (see page 247)
Leaves from a few sprigs of thyme

GLAZED BABY ONIONS:
1 tbsp (15 mL) olive oil
1–2 tbsp (15–30 mL) butter, diced
7 oz (200 g) baby onions, peeled and roots trimmed
1 tsp (5 mL) granulated sugar

BUTTERED VEGETABLES:
5 oz (150 g) baby turnips, trimmed and quartered
5 oz (150 g) baby carrots, trimmed and halved lengthwise
½ large fennel bulb, trimmed and thickly sliced
4 tsp (20 mL) butter
Small handful of chervil leaves, chopped

FOR SERVING:
½ quantity celeriac or turnip purée (see page 250)
4 tsp (20 mL) pesto (see page 249)
5 oz (150 g) cooked baby beets, quartered
Olive oil, for drizzling
Few chives, tarragon leaves, and chervil sprigs, for garnish

TO PREPARE THE CONFIT LAMB, preheat the oven to 275°F (140°C). Trim off the fat and sinew from the shoulder of lamb, then place it in a Dutch oven. Sprinkle with the rock salt, thyme and rosemary sprigs, bay leaf, and garlic cloves. Pour in enough duck fat to cover, then lay a piece of wet parchment paper on top to help keep the lamb submerged in the fat. Heat slowly until the duck fat just begins to simmer. Transfer to the oven and cook slowly until the lamb is very tender, 2½–3 hours. Let the lamb shoulder cool in the fat.

TAKE THE LAMB AND GARLIC out of the fat. Shred the meat using two forks, removing any sinew, and place in a bowl. Squeeze out the soft garlic from the skins and add to the bowl. Moisten the lamb with a few tablespoonfuls of the duck fat and season with salt and pepper to taste.

PLACE A COUPLE OF LAYERS of plastic wrap on a work surface. Shape the confit lamb into a log and wrap up in the plastic. Roll the log on the surface a few times to even out the shape, then chill for a few hours or overnight.

CUT THE LOIN OF LAMB into 12 neat medallions, wrap in plastic wrap, and keep in the fridge until an hour or so before cooking.

FOR THE THYME JUS, boil the lamb jus until reduced by two-thirds or until thickened to a syrupy consistency. Set aside until ready to serve.

FOR THE GLAZED ONIONS, preheat the oven to 350°F (180°C). Heat a stovetop-to-oven skillet, then add the olive oil and butter. Tip in the baby onions and shake the pan to coat them in the foaming butter. Season well and sauté until lightly golden. Sprinkle with the sugar and toss well. Cover the skillet with a piece of parchment paper and place in the oven. Roast, turning occasionally, until the onions are caramelized and tender, 20–25 minutes.

FOR THE BUTTERED VEGETABLES, blanch the baby turnips, carrots, and fennel separately in boiling salted water until tender when pierced with a fine skewer, about 2–2½ minutes. Drain and refresh under cold running water, then drain again and set aside.

WHEN READY TO COOK, unwrap the confit lamb log and slice into rounds about 1¼ inches (3 cm) thick. Heat a skillet and add the 1 tbsp (15 mL) olive oil. Place the confit rounds in the hot pan and fry until golden brown, then carefully turn them over and brown the other side. Remove the pan from the heat and keep the lamb confit warm.

HEAT ANOTHER LARGE SKILLET and add the 1½ tbsp (25 mL) olive oil. Season the lamb medallions with salt and pepper, then fry for 1½–2 minutes on each side—they should feel slightly springy when pressed. Remove to a warm plate and let rest for a few minutes.

TOSS THE BLANCHED VEGETABLES in a hot pan with the butter and chervil over medium heat to warm through. Reheat the lamb jus and add the thyme leaves, along with any juices from the lamb medallions.

TO SERVE, put a tablespoonful of celeriac or turnip purée in the centre of each warm plate and dot a little pesto around. Place the confit lamb on top of the purée. Arrange the lamb medallions, beets, and buttered vegetables on the plates, then pour the lamb jus over them. Drizzle olive oil around and garnish with chives, tarragon, and chervil.

Rack of lamb with confit shoulder, Provençale vegetables, baby spinach, and basil lamb jus

OUR LAMB (FROM CORNWALL IN ENGLAND) HAS A FANTASTIC FLAVOUR AND MELTING TEXTURE. PREPARE THE RACK, CONFIT, AND JUS WELL IN ADVANCE. TO SIMPLIFY THE RECIPE FURTHER, YOU COULD OMIT THE PAN-ROASTED ROOT VEGETABLES AND INSTEAD DOUBLE THE QUANTITY OF FONDANT POTATO. *[Illustrated on page 77]*

Serves 4 as a main course

1 rack of lamb, about 3 lb (1.5 kg)
Few rosemary sprigs
2 tbsp (30 mL) olive oil, plus extra for drizzling
¼ quantity confit of lamb shoulder (see page 190)
4 large basil leaves, finely shredded
4 sun-dried tomatoes in oil, drained and finely chopped
4 olives, pitted and finely chopped
2–3 tbsp (30–45 mL) garlic-infused olive oil
Sea salt and black pepper

BASIL LAMB JUS:
2½ cups (600 mL) lamb jus (see page 247)
Small bunch of basil, leaves finely shredded

PAN-ROASTED ROOT VEGETABLES:
Juice of 1 lemon
1 salsify
1 small head of celeriac
1 small head of kohlrabi
3 tbsp (45 mL) olive oil
1 tbsp (15 mL) butter, diced

FONDANT POTATOES:
1 large (or 2 medium) potato
2 tbsp (30 mL) olive oil
2 tbsp (30 mL) salted butter, diced
7 tbsp (105 mL) vegetable stock (see page 247) or chicken stock (see page 246)

PROVENÇALE VEGETABLES:
2 tbsp (30 mL) olive oil
½ each large red and yellow sweet pepper, seeded and cut into squares
½ small eggplant, trimmed and cut into squares
1 small zucchini, trimmed and cut into squares

FOR SERVING:
Wilted spinach
Celeriac purée (see page 250), optional
2–3 tbsp (30–45 mL) garlic-infused olive oil, for drizzling

TO PREPARE THE LAMB, bone the rack (or ask your butcher to do this for you) and use the bones to make the lamb jus. Trim the meat (which we refer to as a cannon of lamb) into a neat log. Place on a tray, top with the rosemary, and drizzle a little olive oil over. Wrap the tray in plastic wrap and refrigerate.

PUT THE CONFIT LAMB in a bowl and add the basil, tomatoes, and olives. Moisten with the garlic oil and season with salt and pepper to taste. Lay a piece of plastic wrap on a clean surface and spoon the confit lamb on top in a thin cylinder. Press the lamb into a thin log about ¾ inch (2 cm) in diameter, and wrap tightly in the plastic. Chill for a few hours to set the shape.

BOIL THE LAMB JUS until reduced to a syrupy consistency. Set aside.

TO PREPARE THE ROOT VEGETABLES, add the lemon juice to a bowl of water. Peel the salsify, dice, and immediately immerse in the water. Peel the celeriac and kohlrabi and cut into ½-inch (1-cm) cubes. Heat a sauté pan over high heat and add the olive oil. Fry the kohlrabi for 3–4 minutes, then add the celeriac and fry for 2 minutes longer. In the meantime, drain the salsify and pat dry with paper towels. Add to the pan with the butter and fry, tossing frequently, until the vegetables are golden brown and tender, 5–6 minutes. Season well to taste, then keep warm in a low oven.

FOR THE FONDANT POTATOES, peel the potato and cut into discs ⅝ inch (1.5 cm) thick. Heat the olive oil in a large sauté pan. Season the potato and fry for 2 minutes on each side or until golden brown. Pour in the stock and bring to a boil. Dot the potatoes with the butter, then partially cover with a piece of parchment paper. Simmer gently, without turning, until the stock is absorbed and the potatoes are tender, 10–12 minutes. Keep the potatoes warm in a low oven.

WHEN READY TO COOK, preheat the oven to 400°F (200°C). Heat a stovetop-to-oven skillet and add 1 tbsp (15 mL) olive oil. Season the cannon of lamb and fry, turning frequently, until browned all over, 4–5 minutes. Transfer the pan to the oven and roast until the lamb is medium rare, 6–8 minutes. It should feel slightly springy when pressed.

WHILE THE LAMB IS IN THE OVEN, cook the Provençale vegetables: Heat the olive oil in a sauté pan. Season the sweet peppers and eggplant, then add to the pan and sauté for 2 minutes. Add the zucchini, season well, and cook until all the vegetables are just tender, 3–5 minutes longer.

MEANWHILE, heat another skillet with 1 tbsp (15 mL) oil. Unwrap the confit lamb log and cut into ¾-inch (2-cm) pieces. Fry, cut side down, until golden brown, about 2 minutes. Turn over and brown the other side. Remove from the pan and keep warm.

LET THE CANNON OF LAMB REST in a warm place for a few minutes. Reheat the lamb jus and add the basil leaves.

TO SERVE, place a round metal cutter on each warm plate. Spoon in a layer of warm spinach, then a layer of root vegetables. Put one or two slices of potato fondant on top. Cut the cannon of lamb into thick pieces and arrange on top of the potatoes. Arrange the Provençale vegetables and confit lamb around the plates. Add little dollops of celeriac purée, if using, and drizzle with a little garlic-infused olive oil. Serve with the basil lamb jus.

Roasted filet of beef with a truffle and root vegetable infusion

I USE PRIME BEEF FROM NORTHUMBERLAND, IN NORTHEASTERN ENGLAND, FOR THIS DISH. THE TIME-

CONSUMING ELEMENTS ARE THE BRAISED SHANK AND BEEF CONSOMMÉ, BUT YOU CAN MAKE THESE A

DAY AHEAD. IN THE RESTAURANT, WE PREPARE THE INFUSION IN A GLASS TEAPOT WITH AN INFUSER

AND POUR IT OVER THE BEEF AS WE SERVE IT. *[Illustrated on page 82]*

Serves 4–6 as a main course

BRAISED SHANK OF BEEF:
3 tbsp (45 mL) olive oil
1 boned beef shank, in one piece, about 1 lb 5 oz (650 g)
Sea salt and black pepper
1 large carrot, peeled and chopped
1 large onion, peeled and chopped
2 celery stalks, trimmed and chopped
2 bay leaves, few thyme sprigs
2 cups (500 mL) red wine
6 cups (1.5 L) veal stock (see page 247) (approx)

TO CLARIFY THE STOCK:
7 oz (200 g) beef trimmings, chopped
1 thyme sprig, leaves only
1 rosemary sprig, leaves only
4 egg whites
½ tsp (2 mL) black peppercorns

VEGETABLE GARNISH:
½ head of kohlrabi, peeled and diced
Scant 4 oz (100 g) baby carrots, scrubbed and cut into ¼-inch (5-mm) rounds
Scant 2 oz (50 g) shelled green peas
Handful of cooked orrechiette (or other pasta shapes), optional
½ head of Savoy cabbage, shredded and wilted

BEEF FILET:
1 piece of beef filet (tenderloin), about 1 lb (500 g), trimmed
2 tbsp (30 mL) olive oil

TRUFFLE AND ROOT VEGETABLE INFUSION:
2 pea pods, finely sliced
2 asparagus tips, finely sliced lengthwise
2 baby morels, sliced
2 radishes, finely sliced
2 baby carrots, peeled and finely sliced
Small bouquet garni (thyme sprig, rosemary sprig, bay leaf)
Few truffle slices, or 1 tsp (5 mL) truffle trimmings

FOR THE BRAISED SHANK of beef, heat half the olive oil in a large Dutch oven. Season the beef and fry for 2 minutes on each side until evenly browned. Remove to a plate. Add the rest of the oil to the pot, then add the vegetables and herbs. Cook, stirring occasionally, until the vegetables are soft, 4–6 minutes. Deglaze the pan with the wine and boil until reduced by half. Pour in the stock and return the beef to the pot. Add a little water so the beef shank is covered. Bring to a simmer, then turn the heat down. Cover with a piece of wet parchment paper and cook gently until the beef is very tender, 2–3 hours. Remove from the heat and let cool in the braising stock.

TAKE OUT THE BEEF and set aside. Strain the braising stock through a fine chinois into a clean wide pan, pressing down on the vegetables in the chinois with the back of a ladle to extract as much liquid as possible. Place over medium heat and boil the stock until reduced to about 4 cups (1 L). Let cool.

FINELY SHRED THE BEEF and place in a bowl. Add enough stock to moisten the meat and season generously to taste. While still warm, divide into 3½-oz (100-g) portions and place each one in a small resealable plastic bag. Press each bag on the work surface to flatten and use a rolling pin to even out the thickness all over and shape a thin rectangle. Chill overnight, until the beef and gelatinous stock have set.

NEXT, CLARIFY THE STOCK. Put the beef trimmings, herbs, egg whites, and peppercorns into a food processor and blitz for a minute, then tip into the pan containing the cooled beef stock. Slowly bring the stock to a boil, whisking constantly with a balloon whisk. The egg white mix will form a frothy crust on the surface of the liquid. Line a colander with a wet piece of cheesecloth and set it over a large bowl. Ladle the stock into the colander, letting it drip through slowly. It should now be clear; if it is not, repeat the clarification process, using more egg whites. Set this beef consommé aside until ready to serve.

FOR THE VEGETABLE GARNISH, blanch the kohlrabi, carrots, and peas in boiling salted water until just tender, 2–3 minutes. Drain and refresh under cold running water, then set aside.

BEFORE SERVING, remove the shaped braised beef shank from the fridge and bring to room temperature.

TO COOK THE BEEF FILET, preheat the oven to 400°F (200°C). Heat the olive oil in a stovetop-to-oven skillet until hot. Season the beef filet with salt and pepper, then sear, turning, until browned all over. Transfer the skillet to the oven and roast until the meat feels slightly springy when pressed, 4–6 minutes.

MEANWHILE, FOR THE INFUSION, bring the beef consommé to a boil in a pan. Take off the heat and add the sliced vegetables, bouquet garni, and truffle. Cover and let infuse for a few minutes, then strain. Reheat if necessary.

WHEN THE BEEF FILET IS COOKED, remove and let rest in a warm place for a few minutes. Reheat the kohlrabi, carrots, and peas—and pasta, if using— in boiling water for 1–2 minutes.

TO SERVE, put a neat pile of hot cabbage in the centre of each warm plate, using a square metal cutter to create a neat presentation, if you like, then remove the cutter. Unwrap the beef shank and lay it on the cabbage. Pour a little of the consommé over to soften the beef and warm it. Thinly slice the beef filet and place on top of the shank. Arrange the blanched vegetables (and pasta, if using) around the plates. Pour on the remaining beef consommé as you serve.

Slow-braised pork belly with langoustine, crushed peas, and Madeira sauce

IN THE RESTAURANT WE ACCOMPANY THIS DISH WITH LACED PORK CRISPS, MADE BY PRESSING THIN STRIPS OF PORK FAT AND RIND BETWEEN HEAVY TRAYS AND ROASTING THEM UNTIL CRISP. BRAISE THE PORK AND PRESS THE MEAT OVERNIGHT; MAKE THE SAUCE A DAY AHEAD AS WELL—LEAVING YOU AN EASY DISH TO FINISH JUST BEFORE SERVING. *[Illustrated on page 85]*

Serves 4–6 as a main course

BRAISED PORK BELLY:
1 fresh pork belly, about 2¼ lb (1 kg), boned and skinned
Sea salt and black pepper
3 tbsp (45 mL) olive oil
1 large carrot, peeled and chopped
1 onion, peeled and chopped
1 leek, white part only, chopped
1 celery stalk, trimmed and chopped
Few rosemary sprigs
Few thyme sprigs
2 bay leaves
1 cup (250 mL) dry white wine
3 cups (750 mL) veal stock (see page 247)
3 cups (750 mL) chicken stock (see page 246)
2 cups (500 mL) Madeira

CRUSHED PEAS:
2 cups (500 mL) shelled green peas
Small bunch of mint, leaves only
Olive oil, for drizzling

LANGOUSTINE:
8–10 langoustines or scampi, peeled and cleaned, any coral reserved
2 tbsp (30 mL) olive oil

FOR SERVING:
Olive oil, for drizzling

TRIM THE PORK BELLY, reducing the thicker areas to even out the thickness. Rub all over with salt and pepper, then roll up and tie into a neat log. Heat 2 tbsp (30 mL) olive oil in a Dutch oven. Add the pork and fry, turning occasionally, until browned all over, about 8 minutes. Remove and set aside.

DRAIN OFF THE EXCESS OIL and fat from the pot, then add the carrot, onion, leek, celery, and herbs. Stir over high heat until the vegetables take on a little colour and begin to soften, 5–6 minutes. Deglaze the pot with the wine and let bubble until almost totally reduced. Return the pork to the pot. Pour in the veal and chicken stocks and bring to a boil. Reduce the heat to a low simmer and gently braise the pork belly, turning occasionally, until it is very tender, 2½–3 hours. There should be little resistance when a metal skewer is pushed into the centre of the meat.

WHILE STILL HOT, take the pork out of the braising stock and remove the string. Unroll the pork and lay it flat on a large baking sheet. Place another baking sheet on top and weight down with a few heavy cans of food. Let cool completely, then transfer to the fridge and chill for 4–6 hours, or overnight, to set the shape.

PASS THE BRAISING STOCK through a fine sieve into a clean pan, pushing down on the vegetables to extract as much liquid as possible. Bring to a boil and let bubble until reduced by two-thirds.

IN ANOTHER SAUCEPAN, boil the Madeira to reduce by half, then add to the reduced stock. This sauce should have a slightly syrupy consistency; if it seems too thin, boil to reduce and thicken further. Season with salt and pepper to taste.

FOR THE CRUSHED PEAS, add the peas and mint to a pan of boiling water and blanch for 2–3 minutes, then drain and tip into a food processor. Add a generous drizzle of olive oil and pulse for a few seconds until lightly crushed, but not puréed. Season generously with salt and pepper to taste.

WHEN READY TO SERVE, uncover the pork belly and score the fat in a criss-cross pattern, then cut into squares 1–1½ inches (3–4 cm) thick. Rub the langoustine tails with their coral (from the small sac in the head) to enhance their flavour and give them a bright pink coating.

HEAT A HEAVY-BASED SKILLET until very hot, then add 1 tbsp (15 mL) olive oil. Fry the pork squares in batches until golden brown on both sides. Warm up the crushed peas and the Madeira sauce.

HEAT ANOTHER SKILLET and add 2 tbsp (30 mL) olive oil. Season the langoustine tails with salt and pepper and fry for 2 minutes on each side until just cooked. When done, they will turn opaque and feel slightly springy.

TO SERVE, arrange an alternating row of pork belly squares and langoustine tails on each warm serving plate. Place a quenelle of crushed peas at each end. Drizzle a little olive oil and the Madeira sauce around the plates. Serve at once, passing the rest of the Madeira sauce around separately.

Pork cheeks with pork filet wrapped in prosciutto, black pudding, baby turnips, and sautéed morels

THIS IS A REAL CELEBRATION OF THE PIG: SLOW-COOKED PORK CHEEKS, ENCRUSTED IN CRISP POTATO, ARE SERVED WITH PROSCIUTTO-WRAPPED PORK FILETS AND BLACK PUDDING. MAKE THE SAUCE AND PREPARE THE WRAPPED PORK CHEEKS AND FILETS UP TO A DAY AHEAD, LEAVING YOU AN EASY DISH TO ASSEMBLE. *[Illustrated on page 86]*

Serves 4 as a main course

PORK CHEEKS:
8 pork cheeks
Sea salt and black pepper
3 garlic cloves, split (unpeeled)
1 bay leaf
Few thyme sprigs
1¼ lb (625 g) duck or goose fat, melted (approx)
2 large boiling potatoes
Peanut oil, for frying

PORK FILET:
1 pork filet (tenderloin), about 1 lb (500 g)
4 slices of prosciutto (preferably prosciutto di Parma)
1½ tbsp (25 mL) olive oil

BLACK PUDDING AND SAUTÉED MORELS:
Scant 4 oz (100 g) fresh morels, washed and trimmed
1–2 tbsp (15–30 mL) butter, diced
1 tbsp (15 mL) olive oil
7 oz (200 g) black pudding (blood sausage), cut into bite-sized pieces

FOR SERVING:
5 oz (150 g) baby turnips, trimmed and halved
1 quantity Madeira sauce (see page 248)
1 tbsp (15 mL) butter
Wilted spinach
Turnip purée (see page 250), optional

FIRST, CONFIT THE PORK CHEEKS. Season the cheeks and put them in a small saucepan with the garlic, bay leaf, and thyme. Pour in enough duck fat to cover and lay a piece of wet parchment paper that fits snugly on top, to keep the pork cheeks submerged. Place over low heat and cook slowly until soft and tender, 1–1½ hours. Let the pork cheeks cool in the fat.

TRIM THE PORK FILET so that it is evenly thick throughout, then season with salt and pepper. (Use the trimmings to make the Madeira sauce.) Arrange the prosciutto slices on a work surface, overlapping the sides a little to form a sheet. Place the pork filet on one end and roll up, so that the prosciutto wraps around the filet. If you are not cooking immediately, wrap and refrigerate.

REMOVE THE PORK CHEEKS from the fat and pat dry with paper towels. Peel and thinly slice the potatoes using a mandoline. Stack a few slices on top of each other and slice into long strips, then wrap the potato strips around the pork cheeks: To do this, put a thin layer of potato strips on a small piece of plastic wrap, then place a pork cheek on one end. Roll up the plastic wrap to cover the pork cheek with the potatoes. Squeeze gently so that the potato holds together around the meat. Repeat with the remaining pork cheeks and potato. Refrigerate, unless ready to cook.

BLANCH THE BABY TURNIPS in boiling salted water for 3 minutes. Drain and refresh in cold water, then drain again and set aside.

WHEN READY TO COOK, preheat the oven to 400°F (200°C) for the pork filet. Heat a large stovetop-to-oven skillet, then add the olive oil. Fry the prosciutto-wrapped filet, turning occasionally, until browned all over, 3–4 minutes. Transfer the skillet to the oven and roast until just cooked through, 8–10 minutes; the meat should feel just firm. Let rest in a warm place for 5 minutes before slicing.

MEANWHILE, HEAT A THIN LAYER of peanut oil in a skillet. Carefully remove the plastic from the potato-wrapped pork cheeks and place them in the hot pan. Sauté for 2–3 minutes on each side until the potatoes are golden brown and crisp. Tilt the pan slightly and spoon the hot oil over the potatoes as they cook. Drain on paper towels and sprinkle with sea salt. Keep warm.

WHILE THE PORK IS COOKING, add the morels to a hot skillet with the butter. Season and sauté on medium-high heat for 3–4 minutes. Transfer the morels to a warm plate and set aside. Add a little olive oil to the skillet and fry the black pudding for 6–8 minutes, turning occasionally. Warm the Madeira sauce. Toss the baby turnips with butter and some seasoning in a hot pan to heat through. Have the spinach ready.

TO SERVE, PILE THE WARM SPINACH into round metal cutters on warm plates. Add the black pudding and sautéed morels, arranging the mushrooms so that their stemmed sides are facing outward. Remove the cutters. Thickly slice the pork filet and place with the crisp pork cheeks in the centre of the mushrooms. Arrange the turnip halves around the plates and intersperse with little dollops of turnip purée, if using. Spoon the Madeira sauce over the top.

Veal osso bucco with boulangère potatoes, Savoy cabbage, turnip purée, and its own braising jus

OSSO BUCCO MUST BE COOKED VERY GENTLY TO ENSURE A MELTINGLY TENDER RESULT. IN THE RESTAURANT, WE COOK IT IN A SEALED VACUUM PACK IMMERSED IN A WATER BATH FOR 4 HOURS, BUT YOU CAN ACHIEVE AN EXCELLENT RESULT AT HOME PROVIDED YOU MAINTAIN A VERY LOW HEAT—THE SURFACE OF THE LIQUID SHOULD BARELY MOVE. THE OSSO BUCCO TASTES EVEN BETTER IF IT IS MADE A DAY AHEAD. *[Illustrated on page 87]*

Serves 4 as a main course

OSSO BUCCO:

4 veal shank (osso bucco) steaks, about 12 oz (350 g) each, with bone and marrow
Sea salt and black pepper
3 tbsp (45 mL) olive oil
1 large onion, peeled and chopped
1 large carrot, peeled and chopped
3 garlic cloves, peeled and sliced
1 bay leaf
Few thyme sprigs
1 tbsp (15 mL) tomato paste
Scant 1 cup (200 mL) dry white wine
3¼ cups (800 mL) veal stock (see page 247)

POMMES BOULANGÈRE:

1 cup (250 mL) chicken stock (see page 246)
5 garlic cloves, peeled
Few thyme sprigs
Few rosemary sprigs
2 tbsp (30 mL) olive oil, plus extra for brushing
2 large shallots, peeled and finely chopped
7 oz (200 g) potatoes (about 4 medium)
2 tbsp (30 mL) butter, diced

GLAZED BABY ONIONS:

1 tbsp (15 mL) olive oil
1 tbsp (15 mL) butter
7 oz (200 g) baby onions, peeled and roots trimmed
1 tsp (5 mL) granulated sugar

FOR SERVING:

About ½ head of Savoy cabbage, cored and shredded
Scant 2 oz (50 g) trompette de la mort (or other fresh wild mushrooms), cleaned
1 tbsp (15 mL) olive oil
1–2 tbsp (15–30 mL) butter, diced
Turnip purée (see page 250)
Olive oil, for drizzling

FOR THE OSSO BUCCO, season the veal pieces. Heat a wide pan or Dutch oven, then add half the olive oil and brown the veal for 2 minutes on each side. Transfer to a plate. Add a little more oil to the pan and tip in the chopped vegetables, garlic, and herbs. Fry the vegetables until soft, 4–6 minutes. Add the tomato paste and stir for 2 minutes. Pour in the wine, scraping the bottom of the pan to deglaze. Let the wine bubble until reduced by half. Add the veal stock and return the browned veal to the pan. If needed, add a little water so the veal is covered. Lay a piece of wet parchment paper on top of the veal to keep it submerged in the liquid. Turn the heat right down and leave to simmer very gently until tender, 1½–2 hours.

FOR THE POMMES BOULANGÈRE, preheat the oven to 400°F (200°C). Pour the chicken stock into a pan. Crush 2 garlic cloves and add to the stock with the herbs. Bring to a boil and boil for 2 minutes, then remove from the heat and let infuse for 10 minutes. Brush an ovenproof dish with olive oil. Finely chop the remaining 3 garlic cloves. Heat a little olive oil in a small skillet and gently sauté the garlic with the shallots until softened and lightly coloured, 4–6 minutes. In the meantime, peel and finely slice the potatoes using a mandoline.

LAYER THE POTATOES in the dish, overlapping the slices and sprinkling each layer with sautéed shallots, garlic, and plenty of seasoning. Finish with a final layer of potatoes. Strain the infused stock and pour enough into the potato dish to come two-thirds of the way up the sides. Press down on the potatoes slightly, then dot the butter all over the top. Place in the oven and bake until the potatoes are golden brown on top and feel tender when pierced with a skewer, 30–40 minutes. Keep warm.

FOR THE GLAZED BABY ONIONS, lower the oven setting to 350°F (180°C). Heat a stovetop-to-oven sauté pan, then add the olive oil and butter, followed by the baby onions. Shake the pan to coat the onions in the foaming butter, season well, and sauté until the onions are lightly golden. Sprinkle with the sugar and toss well. Cover the pan with a piece of parchment paper and transfer to the oven. Roast the onions, turning them occasionally, until they have caramelized and are tender all the way through, 20–25 minutes.

MEANWHILE, BLANCH THE SAVOY CABBAGE in boiling salted water for 1 minute, then drain and refresh in cold water. Drain and set aside.

REMOVE THE VEAL from the braising stock and set aside. Strain the stock through a fine sieve into a clean pan, pressing down on the vegetables with the back of a ladle to extract all the liquid. Boil the stock until it has reduced down to a thick and syrupy sauce. Taste and adjust the seasoning.

WHEN READY TO SERVE, sauté the mushrooms with the olive oil and a few dice of butter until softened. Reheat the veal in the sauce for a few minutes. Sauté the cabbage with a few dice of butter until just tender. Place a round metal cutter on each warm plate and spoon in a layer of cabbage. Arrange the mushrooms in a circle around the plate. Place little dollops of turnip purée at intervals and top with the glazed baby onions. Remove the cutters and place the veal on top of the cabbage. Drizzle the reduced braising stock over the veal and drizzle a little olive oil around the plates. Slice the pomme boulangère into portions and serve alongside.

Risotto of cèpes with green onions, grated truffle, and parmesan

THIS IS AN IDEAL MAIN COURSE FOR VEGETARIANS, AND CAN ALSO BE SERVED IN SMALLER PORTIONS AS AN APPETIZER. RATHER THAN MAKE RISOTTO THE LABORIOUS, TRADITIONAL WAY, I BLANCH MY RICE IN ADVANCE, WHICH HALVES THE LAST-MINUTE COOKING TIME. THE RESULT IS JUST AS DELICIOUSLY RICH AND CREAMY, PROVIDED YOU USE A GOOD RISOTTO RICE. *[Illustrated on page 89]*

Serves 4 as a main course

SAUTÉED CÈPES:
8 oz (250 g) fresh cèpes (porcini), cleaned
2 tbsp (30 mL) olive oil, plus extra for brushing
Sea salt and black pepper
1–2 tbsp (15–30 mL) butter, diced

RISOTTO:
1 heaped cup (heaped 250 mL) risotto rice (such as carnaroli or vialone nano)
2½ cups (600 ml) vegetable stock (see page 247), approx
⅓ oz (10 g) dried cèpes (porcini), rinsed
4 tbsp (60 mL) olive oil
2 large shallots, peeled and finely chopped
7 tbsp (105 ml) dry white wine
2 tbsp (30 mL) mascarpone
2 tbsp (30 mL) freshly grated parmesan
2 green onions (green part only), finely chopped
4 tsp (20 mL) butter

FOR SERVING:
Fresh truffle slices, for garnish
Few parsley crisps (see page 248)
Truffle-infused olive oil, for drizzling

HALVE 2 LARGE CÈPES. Chop the rest, and set all the mushrooms aside until ready to cook.

FOR THE RISOTTO, bring a large pan of salted water to a boil. Add the rice and blanch the grains for 5 minutes. Drain well and spread out on a lightly oiled tray. Let cool, then cover with plastic wrap and set aside until ready to cook and serve. (If preparing several hours ahead, refrigerate.)

PUT THE STOCK in another saucepan with the dried cèpes. Bring to a boil, then remove from the heat and let infuse for 10–15 minutes. Strain the stock and return to the pan. (You could use the cèpes for another dish.)

WHEN READY TO COOK, heat 2 tbsp (30 mL) olive oil a saucepan and add the shallots. Stir over medium heat until beginning to soften, 3–4 minutes. Add the blanched rice and cook, stirring, for 1–2 minutes, then pour in the wine. Let bubble until almost totally reduced. Add one-third of the infused stock and cook, stirring occasionally, until the rice has absorbed almost all the stock. Add another third of the stock and simmer, stirring from time to time, until the liquid is nearly all absorbed. Pour in half of the remaining stock and simmer, stirring, until it has been absorbed.

NOW TASTE THE RICE to see if it is al dente. Add a splash more stock if the grains are still a little chalky. Remove the pan from the heat.

HEAT A RIDGED CAST-IRON GRILL PAN until hot. Brush the halved cèpes with a little olive oil and season well. Put them on the grill pan and cook until nicely charred and tender, 4–5 minutes. Heat the rest of the oil in a large skillet and add the chopped cèpes with a few dice of butter. Season well and sauté over high heat until lightly browned and tender, 3–4 minutes.

RETURN THE RISOTTO to a gentle heat and add a little more stock. Stir in the sautéed chopped cèpes, followed by the mascarpone, parmesan, green onions, and, finally, the butter. Taste and adjust the seasoning.

DIVIDE THE RISOTTO among warm bowls and top each serving with a pan-grilled cèpe half. Garnish with the truffle slices and parsley crisps. Drizzle a little truffle-infused oil over the top and serve immediately.

DESSERTS

Caramelized pear tatin with
gorgonzola ice cream and
walnut cream

[Recipe on page 208]

Caramelized apple tarte tatin
with vanilla ice cream

[Recipe on page 210]

Carrot and white chocolate fondant
with dark chocolate sorbet

[Recipe on page 212]

Toffee soufflé
with banana and lime ice cream

[Recipe on page 214]

Lemon meringue
with marinated strawberries

[Recipe on page 216]

Plum crumble tart
with almond frangipane

[Recipe on page 218]

Raspberry compote
with tarragon cream

[Recipe on page 220]

Pineapple ravioli with mango filling,
berries, and mint sorbet

[Recipe on page 222]

Pineapple and chili soup
with fromage blanc foam

[Recipe on page 224]

Sablé breton with raspberries, vanilla cream, and vanilla ice cream

[Recipe on page 226]

Tiramisu with coffee granita

[Recipe on page 228]

Raspberry, lemon, and basil millefeuille with milk ice cream

[Recipe on page 230]

Palet d'or with chocolate and hazelnut ice cream and passion fruit cream

[Recipe on page 232]

Slow-baked quince with crème catalan, Pedro Ximenez gelée, and acacia honey granita

[Recipe on page 234]

Chocolate parfait with passion fruit and guava coulis

[Recipe on page 236]

Bitter chocolate mousse with coffee granita and light ginger cream

[Recipe on page 238]

Apple parfait with honeycomb, bitter chocolate, and champagne foam

[Recipe on page 241]

Caramelized pear tatin with gorgonzola ice cream and walnut

cream IN THE RESTAURANT WE MAKE INDIVIDUAL TATINS IN SMALL SHALLOW SKILLETS, BUT

YOU CAN MAKE A LARGE TART USING A SAUTÉ PAN OR AN 8-INCH (20-CM) TATIN MOULD INSTEAD.

GORGONZOLA ICE CREAM IS AN IDEAL PARTNER, BUT YOU COULD SERVE THE TATIN WITH A SIMPLE

VANILLA ICE CREAM, IF YOU PREFER. [Illustrated on page 93]

Serves 6

GORGONZOLA ICE CREAM:
1 cup (250 mL) milk
1 cup (250 mL) whipping cream
6 egg yolks
½ cup (125 mL) granulated sugar
4 oz (125 g) gorgonzola, crumbled

WALNUT CREAM:
1 cup (250 mL) whipping cream
2 tbsp (30 mL) granulated sugar
Scant ½ cup (scant 125 mL) chopped, skinned, and lightly toasted walnuts

PEAR TATIN:
6 Bartlett pears
1 lb (500 g) puff pastry
⅔ cup (150 mL) unsalted butter
¾ cup (175 mL) granulated sugar

FOR SERVING:
Reduced light caramel, for drizzling (optional)
6 dried pear slices (see page 251), optional

FIRST, MAKE THE ICE CREAM. Put the milk and cream into a saucepan and slowly bring to a boil. Meanwhile, beat the egg yolks and sugar together in a large bowl. As the creamy milk begins to boil, slowly pour it onto the yolk and sugar mix, whisking constantly. Strain through a fine sieve into a clean pan.

RETURN TO LOW HEAT and stir constantly with a wooden spoon until slightly thickened, to form a light custard sauce. Add the crumbled cheese and stir until it melts and the custard is smooth. Let cool completely, stirring every once in a while to prevent a skin from forming on the surface. Pour into an ice-cream machine and churn until almost firm. Transfer the ice cream to a shallow container and freeze for a few hours, or overnight, until firm.

FOR THE WALNUT CREAM, put the cream and sugar in a saucepan and stir over low heat until the sugar has dissolved. Increase the heat. When the liquid is almost boiling, remove from the heat and tip in the walnuts. Let infuse and cool slightly for 10 minutes. Blitz the creamy walnut infusion in a blender until smooth, then pass through a fine sieve into a bowl, pressing down on the pulp in the sieve with the back of a spoon. Using an electric mixer, whip the cream to soft peaks, then cover and chill until ready to serve.

FOR THE PEAR TATINS, have ready six 3½-inch (9-cm) diameter shallow cake pans that can be used on top of the stove, or stovetop-to-oven skillets. Peel and halve the pears, then scoop out the cores, using a melon baller. Lay the pear halves on a tray lined with paper towels and pat off moisture with more paper towels. Let dry, uncovered, for a few hours, or chill overnight if possible—it won't matter if the pears discolour, because they'll be coated in caramel.

ROLL OUT THE PUFF PASTRY thinly on a lightly floured surface. Cut out six rounds that are slightly larger than the diameter of the pans. Lay the pastry discs on a tray lined with parchment paper. Cover and chill while you prepare the pears and caramel.

CUT THE BUTTER INTO THIN SLICES. Scatter over the bottom of the cake pans and sprinkle the sugar on top. Place the pans over medium heat to melt the butter and sugar and form a light caramel. Add the pears and cook until the caramel turns deep amber and the pears are golden brown, about 8 minutes. Remove from the heat and let cool.

REARRANGE THE PEARS as necessary, so they are cut side up in the pans. Carefully drape the puff pastry discs over the pears and tuck the edges down inside the pans. (At this stage, the tatins can be kept in the fridge for a few hours, ready for baking half an hour before serving.)

WHEN READY TO COOK, preheat the oven to 400°F (200°C). Place the tatins in the oven and bake until the pastry is golden brown and crisp, 20–25 minutes. Let cool slightly.

TO SERVE, drizzle individual serving plates decoratively with a little reduced caramel, if you like. Carefully unmould the pear tatins, upside down, onto the plates. Place a scoop of gorgonzola ice cream and a spoonful of walnut cream on each plate and decorate with dried pear slices, if using.

Caramelized apple tarte tatin with vanilla ice cream

THIS ELEGANT DESSERT IS DESIGNED TO SERVE TWO, BUT YOU CAN EASILY MAKE AN EXTRA TATIN OR TWO TO SERVE MORE; THERE IS ENOUGH ICE CREAM FOR 5–6 PORTIONS. VANILLA BEANS DUSTED WITH ICING SUGAR PROVIDE THE PERFECT FINISHING TOUCH–DRY THE EMPTY PODS AFTER YOU HAVE MADE THE ICE CREAM, TO USE FOR THE DECORATION. *[Illustrated on page 95]*

Serves 2

APPLE TATIN:
3 large, crisp apples
8 oz (250 g) puff pastry
¼ cup (50 mL) cold unsalted butter
¼ cup (50 mL) granulated sugar

VANILLA ICE CREAM:
1 cup (250 mL) whipping cream
1 cup (250 mL) milk
2 vanilla beans, split lengthwise
6 egg yolks
½ cup (125 mL) granulated sugar

FOR SERVING:
2–3 vanilla beans (seeds removed), sliced lengthwise
Icing sugar, for dusting

TO PREPARE THE APPLES, peel, core, and quarter them, then lay them on a tray lined with paper towels. Let dry, uncovered, for 2–3 hours, or preferably chill overnight. Don't worry if they turn brown; they will be coated in caramel.

NEXT, MAKE THE ICE CREAM. Pour the cream and milk into a pan. Scrape out the seeds from the vanilla beans and add them to the pan with the empty pods. Slowly bring to a boil. Meanwhile, beat the egg yolks and sugar together in a large bowl. As the creamy milk begins to boil, slowly pour it onto the yolk and sugar mix, whisking all the time. Strain through a fine sieve into a clean pan.

STIR THE CUSTARD over low heat with a wooden spoon until it thickens enough to lightly coat the back of the spoon. Let cool completely, stirring every once in a while to prevent a skin from forming. Pass the cooled custard through a fine sieve (removing and reserving the vanilla pods), then pour it into an ice-cream machine and churn until thick and smooth. Transfer the ice cream to a plastic container and freeze for a few hours, or overnight, until firm.

FOR THE TARTE TATIN, have ready an 8-inch (20-cm) shallow cake pan that can be used on top of the stove, or a stovetop-to-oven skillet.

ROLL OUT THE PASTRY THINLY on a lightly floured surface and cut out a 9½-inch (24-cm) round, using a similar-sized plate as a guide. Lift onto a rimless baking sheet and chill while you prepare the filling.

CUT THE BUTTER INTO THIN SLICES and scatter over the bottom of the cake pan or skillet. Sprinkle with the sugar. Arrange the apple quarters neatly around the pan, with one in the middle. Place over medium heat to melt the butter and sugar and form a light caramel. Carefully shake the pan from time to time to insure that the apples are well coated with the caramel and are evenly brown. Let cool slightly.

WHEN READY TO COOK, preheat the oven to 400°F (200°C). Drape the pastry over the apples and carefully tuck the edges down inside the pan. Place the pan in the hot oven and bake for 15 minutes. Lower the oven setting to 350°F (180°C) and bake until the pastry is golden brown and crisp, 15–20 minutes longer. Let cool.

TO SERVE, dust the sliced vanilla pods liberally with icing sugar, shaking off excess. Unmould the tarte tatin, upside down, onto a serving plate, top with the sugar-dusted vanilla, and serve with scoops of vanilla ice cream.

Carrot and white chocolate fondant with dark chocolate sorbet

THE COMBINATION OF FLAVOURS IN THESE PUDDINGS IS TRULY DELICIOUS. IF YOU DO NOT HAVE THE

CYLINDRICAL MOULDS DESCRIBED, USE METAL PANNACOTTA OR DARIOLE MOULDS, MAKING SURE THAT

THE CENTRES ARE WELL CONTAINED WITHIN THE CAKE BATTER, OTHERWISE THE PUDDINGS WILL NOT

HOLD UP. PREPARE THE SORBET, CARROT PURÉE, AND CENTRES WELL IN ADVANCE. *[Illustrated on page 98]*

Serves about 10–12

DARK CHOCOLATE SORBET:

7 oz (200 g) dark, bitter chocolate (approx 75% cocoa solids)
2/3 cup (150 mL) whipping cream
1/2 cup (125 mL) granulated sugar

CARROT PURÉE:

1 lb (500 g) carrots, peeled
3 cups (750 mL) fresh carrot juice (prepared with a juicer, or store-bought)

SOFT CENTRES:

Generous 2/3 cup (160mL) whipping cream
1 oz (30 g) white chocolate

CAKE BATTER:

2½ oz (75 g) good-quality white chocolate
1/3 cup (75 mL) unsalted butter, plus extra for brushing
5 extra large egg yolks
2/3 cup (150 mL) ground almonds
Pinch of ground cinnamon
4½ tbsp (67 mL) rice flour
1/4 cup (50 mL) finely chopped walnuts
4 oz (120 g) egg whites (from about 3 extra large eggs)
2/3 cup (150 mL) superfine sugar

FIRST, MAKE THE SORBET. Chop the dark chocolate and place in a heatproof bowl. Combine the cream, sugar, and 1¾ cups (400 mL) water in a saucepan and stir over low heat until the sugar has dissolved. Bring to a boil, then immediately pour onto the chocolate, stirring constantly. Continue to stir until the chocolate has melted and the mixture is smooth. Pass through a fine sieve into a bowl and let cool completely. Pour into an ice-cream machine and churn until almost firm. Transfer to a suitable container and freeze for a few hours, or overnight, until firm.

TO MAKE THE CARROT PURÉE, roughly chop the carrots and place in a saucepan with the carrot juice. Cover with a piece of wet parchment paper and bring to a boil. Cook until the carrots are very soft and the liquid has reduced by half, 15–20 minutes. Transfer the carrots and juice to a blender and blitz to a fine, smooth purée; it should be quite firm, not runny. Measure out 10 oz (300 g) of the purée and set aside for the soft molten centres.

PUT THE REMAINING CARROT PURÉE in a clean pan and cook over medium heat for 15–20 minutes, stirring frequently, to reduce and dry out a little. Let cool. Measure 4 oz (110 g) reduced carrot purée for the cake batter and set aside. (Use any remaining purée for another dish.)

TO PREPARE THE SOFT CENTRES, put the cream into a saucepan and slowly bring to a boil. Meanwhile, chop the white chocolate into small pieces and put into a heatproof bowl. As soon as the cream begins to boil, pour onto the white chocolate, stirring until the mixture is smooth. Let cool slightly, then mix in the reserved 10 oz (300 g) carrot purée. Pour the mixture into a shallow plastic container and freeze for a few hours, or overnight, until firm.

FOR THE CAKE, preheat the oven to 350°F (180°C). Line the bottom of 10–12 straight-sided cylindrical moulds, about 1½ inches (4 cm) in diameter and 2½ inches (6 cm) in height, with parchment paper discs. Brush these and the sides of the moulds with soft butter. Stand the prepared moulds on a rimmed baking sheet and set aside. Remove the frozen carrot and white chocolate mixture from the freezer and set aside to soften slightly in a cool part of the kitchen while you make the cake batter.

CHOP THE WHITE CHOCOLATE and place in a heatproof bowl with the butter. Set over a pan of barely simmering water to melt. Stir until the mixture is smooth, then remove from the heat. Gradually add the 4 oz (110 g) reduced carrot purée, stirring until smooth, then incorporate the egg yolks. Mix together the ground almonds, cinnamon, rice flour, and chopped walnuts, then fold into the carrot mixture.

IN A CLEAN, DRY BOWL, beat the egg whites with an electric mixer to soft peaks. Beat in the sugar, a tablespoonful at a time, and continue to beat until the meringue is firm and shiny. Carefully fold into the carrot batter.

WORKING FAST, use a round metal cutter (about ⅝–¾ inch/1.5–2 cm in diameter and 1¼ inches/3 cm deep) to stamp out little cylinders from the frozen carrot and white chocolate centres. Put 1–2 tbsp (15–30 mL) of cake batter into each prepared mould, then carefully place a carrot and chocolate cylinder on top. Spoon 1–2 tbsp (15–30 mL) of cake batter over each cylinder to cover it and fill up the mould. Bake until the tops of the fondants are golden brown, 20–25 minutes. (Remove from the oven immediately if the tops look as though they are about to burst open to reveal the filling.)

HOLDING EACH MOULD with a cloth to protect your hands, run a small, thin knife around the side of the fondant, then invert onto a serving plate and remove the mould. Place a quenelle of chocolate sorbet alongside and serve.

Toffee soufflé with banana and lime ice cream

A SOUFFLÉ NEVER FAILS TO IMPRESS. JUST MAKE SURE YOU HAVE EVERYTHING READY AND WAITING THE MOMENT YOU TAKE THE DISHES FROM THE OVEN—SERVING PLATES, ICE CREAM, AND GUESTS. MAKE THE SOUFFLÉ BASE, NOUGATINE, AND ICE CREAM WELL AHEAD, READY TO WHIP UP THE MERINGUE AND FOLD IT INTO THE SOUFFLÉ BASE AT THE LAST MINUTE. *[Illustrated on page 99]*

Serves about 8

SOUFFLÉ BASE:

3 tbsp (45 mL) butter, softened to room temperature, plus extra for brushing

7 tbsp (105 mL) all-purpose flour

Pinch of fine sea salt

3 extra large egg yolks

⅔ cup (150 mL) milk

7 tbsp (105 mL) granulated sugar

NOUGATINE:

¾ cup (175 mL) granulated sugar

⅓ cup (75 mL) toasted sliced almonds

BANANA AND LIME ICE CREAM:

2 cups (500 mL) whole milk

2 cups (500 mL) whipping cream

1 vanilla bean, split lengthwise (optional)

8 extra large egg yolks

1¾ cups (425 mL) granulated sugar

3 medium bananas

4 tbsp (60 mL) crème de banane liqueur

7 tbsp (105 mL) lime juice (from 2–3 limes)

MERINGUE:

8 extra large egg whites

6 tbsp (90 mL) superfine sugar

FOR THE SOUFFLÉ BASE, in a large bowl, beat 1 tbsp (15 mL) butter with the flour, salt, and egg yolks to a thick paste. Heat the milk in a saucepan to just below a boil, then gradually beat into the paste a little at a time until the mixture is smooth. Pass through a fine sieve back into the pan, pushing it through with the back of a spoon. Stir over low heat until the mixture is very thick, about 3 minutes. Transfer to a food processor and blitz until very smooth. Leave in the processor while you make the toffee.

MELT THE SUGAR in a heavy-based pan over high heat, swirling the pan as the sugar begins to melt at the edges. When it forms a dark caramel, take the pan off the heat and carefully add the remaining butter, shaking the pan to mix the caramel with the butter.

WITH THE MOTOR RUNNING, slowly pour the toffee onto the soufflé base in the processor, blending until well mixed. Transfer to a large bowl and let cool if not using immediately. (The soufflé base can be kept in the fridge for 2–3 days.)

FOR THE NOUGATINE, melt the sugar in a heavy-based pan, swirling the pan as the sugar melts and caramelizes. When it is a terracotta colour, mix in the almonds. Immediately pour onto a non-stick baking sheet (or lined with a silicone baking mat). Tilt the sheet to level the nut caramel and let cool until firm and brittle, about 15 minutes.

BREAK UP THE NOUGATINE, then finely chop with a heavy knife. Store in an airtight container until ready to use.

FOR THE BANANA ICE CREAM, make the crème anglaise: Pour the milk and cream into a heavy-based pan. If using vanilla, scrape the seeds into the creamy milk and add the pod, too. Slowly bring to just below a boil. Meanwhile, beat the egg yolks and 1¼ cups (300 mL) of the sugar together in a large bowl. Slowly pour the creamy milk onto the eggs and sugar, whisking continuously. Strain through a fine sieve into a clean pan and stir with a wooden spoon over low heat until the crème anglaise has thickened enough to lightly coat the back of the spoon. Pour into a bowl and cool quickly over another bowl of ice water, stirring the crème anglaise occasionally to prevent a skin from forming.

FINELY PURÉE 2 BANANAS in a blender (you need 7 oz/200 g purée); roughly chop the other banana. Heat the rest of the sugar in a non-stick skillet until melted and turned to a light caramel. Add the chopped banana and toss over high heat to caramelize. Take off the heat and stir in the banana purée, crème de banane, and lime juice. Return to the heat and stir until smooth. Tip into the crème anglaise and use an immersion blender to combine the mixtures. Transfer to an ice-cream machine and churn until almost firm. Scoop into a shallow container and freeze until firm.

HALF AN HOUR BEFORE SERVING, warm up the soufflé base by placing the bowl in a large pan half-filled with warm water. Leave for 20 minutes.

PREHEAT THE OVEN to 375°F (190°C). Brush eight 1¼-cup (300-ml) individual soufflé dishes (about 2⅝ inches/6.5 cm deep and 4 inches/9.5 cm in diameter) with soft butter. Chill until firm, then brush with another layer of butter. Dust with chopped nougatine and shake out any excess; reserve. Place a heavy rimless baking sheet in the oven to heat up.

FOR THE MERINGUE, beat the egg whites in a clean, dry bowl until stiff, then whisk in the sugar, a tablespoonful at a time, until fully incorporated and the meringue holds soft peaks. Using a large metal spoon, fold the meringue into the soufflé base. Spoon the mixture into the prepared dishes until almost full. Run a knife around the top edge of the dishes, then sprinkle any remaining crushed nougatine on top. Stand the dishes on the hot baking sheet and bake for about 10 minutes. The soufflés are ready when they are golden brown and feel a little springy when lightly pressed. (If your oven is too hot and the soufflés look as though they are about to crack in the middle, take them out.)

STAND THE SOUFFLÉ DISHES on individual serving plates with a little dish of banana and lime ice cream alongside. Serve immediately.

Lemon meringue with marinated strawberries

AT THE RESTAURANT, WE BAKE MERINGUES IN A STEAM OVEN TO GET A SOFT CENTRE. HERE, THEY ARE PARTLY COOKED IN THE MICROWAVE, THEN BAKED BRIEFLY IN A HOT OVEN TO ACHIEVE A SIMILAR RESULT. BLACK PEPPER AND SESAME TUILES ARE PERFECT WITH THIS DESSERT, BUT YOU CAN SERVE IT WITH ANY CRISP DESSERT COOKIES. *[Illustrated on page 100]*

Serves 8–10

STRAWBERRY SORBET:
1 lb (500 g) ripe strawberries, hulled
Juice of 1 large lemon
1 cup (250 mL) granulated sugar
1½ tbsp (25 mL) liquid glucose or light corn syrup

BLACK PEPPER AND SESAME TUILES:
⅔ cup (150 mL) icing sugar
3 tbsp (45 mL) all-purpose flour
¼ cup (50 mL) lightly salted butter, melted
3 tbsp (45 mL) white sesame seeds
Cracked black pepper, for sprinkling

LEMON MERINGUE:
3½ oz (100 g) egg whites (from 2–3 extra large eggs)
6 tbsp (90 mL) superfine sugar
Finely grated rind of 2 lemons
Icing sugar, for dusting

VANILLA OIL:
Seeds from ½ vanilla bean
4 tbsp (60 mL) olive oil

FOR SERVING:
8 oz (250 g) strawberries (ideally including some fraises des bois), hulled and larger ones halved
Good-quality aged balsamic vinegar, for drizzling
Handful of small basil leaves

FIRST, MAKE THE SORBET. Put the strawberries and lemon juice into a food processor and blitz to a smooth purée. Tip into a saucepan, bring to a boil, and let bubble until reduced by half. Cool slightly, then rub the purée through a fine sieve to remove the seeds. Let the purée cool completely.

FOR THE SORBET SYRUP put the sugar and scant 1 cup (200 mL) water in a heavy-based saucepan. Add the liquid glucose and heat gently until the sugar has dissolved. Increase the heat and boil the syrup for 5 minutes until slightly thickened. Cool completely, then mix with the strawberry purée. Pour the mixture into an ice-cream machine and churn until almost firm. Transfer to a suitable container and freeze until firm.

TO MAKE THE TUILES, preheat the oven to 350°F (180°C) and line a rimless baking sheet with a silicone baking mat. Sift the icing sugar into a bowl. Add 4 tsp (20 mL) water and stir until well blended. Mix in the flour. Stir in the melted butter and then the sesame seeds.

SPREAD 1–2 TBSP (15–30 ML) of the batter on the prepared baking sheet. Place a large piece of parchment paper on top and roll out the batter thinly, using a rolling pin. Carefully peel off the parchment and sprinkle black pepper over the tuile. Bake until golden brown, 6–8 minutes. Let cool on the baking sheet for 1 minute only.

WHILE THE TUILE IS STILL WARM and pliable, cut it into strips about ⅝ inch (1.5 cm) wide and 3½ inches (9 cm) long. If it becomes too brittle to cut, return to the oven for a minute to soften slightly. The tuile will crisp up once cooled. Repeat, using the rest of the batter, to make more tuiles. Store in an airtight container, separating the layers with parchment paper.

FOR THE LEMON MERINGUE, preheat the oven to 400°F (200°C). Line a non-metal tray (suitable to go in a microwave) with parchment paper. Put the egg whites into a large clean bowl (or the bowl of an electric mixer). Beat slowly to begin with, then increase the speed to high and beat until the egg whites form soft peaks. Gradually beat in the sugar, a tablespoonful at a time, until fully incorporated and the meringue is smooth and glossy. Do not over-beat; stop if the meringue begins to look grainy around the edges. Finally, carefully fold in the grated lemon rind.

PIPE THE MERINGUE IN BATCHES: Spoon into a disposable pastry bag and cut off the tip to create an opening about 1½ inches (3.5 cm) in diameter. Pipe thick straight lines, about 4 inches (10 cm) in length, onto the lined tray. Gently pat down the peaked ends of each meringue with a wet finger. Microwave on the highest setting for 20 seconds. Remove and slide the parchment onto a rimless baking sheet.

DUST THE MERINGUES heavily with icing sugar, then bake in the oven until lightly golden, about 3 minutes. The meringues should feel a little crisp on the outside where the sugar has caramelized, with a soft, marshmallowy centre.

FOR THE VANILLA OIL, mix the vanilla seeds with the olive oil.

WHEN READY TO SERVE, trim the ends of the meringues diagonally, then use a metal spatula to carefully lift them onto individual serving plates. Arrange the strawberries on both sides and drizzle with a little balsamic vinegar. Scatter the basil leaves around the berries and drizzle a little vanilla oil around each plate. Add a scoop of strawberry sorbet and a tuile to each plate and serve immediately, with the rest of the tuiles passed around separately.

Plum crumble tart with almond frangipane

MAKE ALL THE DIFFERENT COMPONENTS OF THIS DESSERT A DAY IN ADVANCE, READY TO ASSEMBLE AND BAKE A FEW HOURS BEFORE SERVING. I LOVE THIS DRAMATIC PRESENTATION, BUT YOU COULD SIMPLY SPOON THE PLUM SAUCE AROUND THE TARTS TO SAVE TIME. *[Illustrated on page 101]*

Makes about 10

PASTRY:
Scant 8 oz (225 g) all-purpose flour (about 1²/₃ cups/400 mL)
Pinch of fine sea salt
1 tsp (5 mL) granulated sugar
²/₃ cup (150 mL) unsalted butter, diced
1 large egg yolk, beaten with 2¹/₂ tbsp (37 mL) water

FRANGIPANE:
¹/₃ cup (75 mL) unsalted butter, softened to room temperature
6 tbsp (90 mL) granulated sugar
1 extra large egg, lightly beaten
³/₄ cup (175 mL) finely ground almonds

PLUM FILLING AND SAUCE:
12 firm (slightly under-ripe) plums
4 cups (1 L) stock syrup (see page 251)

PLUM PURÉE:
3 plums
2 tbsp (30 mL) granulated sugar

CRUMBLE:
6 tbsp (90 mL) all-purpose flour
Pinch of fine sea salt
3 tbsp (45 mL) unsalted butter, diced
3 tbsp (45 mL) granulated sugar
Scant ¹/₂ cup (scant 125 mL) finely ground almonds

TO ASSEMBLE:
Icing sugar, for dusting
Bittersweet chocolate, melted, for decoration

FOR SERVING:
Clotted cream or vanilla ice cream (see page 251)

FOR THE PASTRY, sift the flour and salt into a bowl and stir in the sugar. Put into a food processor along with the butter and blitz until the mixture resembles coarse crumbs. Add the beaten egg and pulse for a few seconds until the mixture comes together. Tip onto a lightly floured surface, gather into a ball, and knead for a minute or so until smooth; avoid overworking the dough. Wrap in plastic wrap and let rest in the fridge for about 30 minutes before rolling out.

FOR THE FRANGIPANE, beat the butter and sugar together in a bowl until pale and creamy. Incorporate the egg and, finally, the ground almonds. Cover the bowl with plastic wrap and set aside.

FOR THE PLUM FILLING, halve and pit 8 plums, then cut into wedges. Place in a small saucepan with the stock syrup over low heat and gently poach the plums until softened but still holding their shape, 6–8 minutes. With a slotted spoon, transfer to a bowl and let cool. Reserve the syrup.

FOR THE SAUCE, halve and pit the remaining 4 plums and cut into wedges. Poach in the reserved stock syrup for 8–10 minutes until soft. Transfer to a blender with 2–3 tbsp of the poaching syrup and blend to a smooth purée. Push the purée through a fine sieve into a bowl and add a little more of the syrup if the sauce is too thick. Cool, then pour into a plastic squeezy bottle. Reserve the rest of the poaching syrup.

FOR THE PLUM PURÉE, halve, pit, and roughly chop the plums. Toss with the sugar and place in a large non-stick skillet. Cook over medium heat until the plums are softened and any juices have evaporated. If the pan looks too dry and the sugar begins to caramelize, add 1–2 tbsp (15–30 mL) of the poaching syrup. When soft, tip the plums into a blender and blend to a smooth purée. Transfer to a bowl and let cool.

PREHEAT THE OVEN to 400°F (200°C). Roll out the pastry on a lightly floured surface and use to line 3-inch (8-cm) tartlet moulds (preferably moulds with removable bases. Chill for 20 minutes. Line the tartlet shells with parchment paper and baking beans, and bake for 15 minutes. Remove the beans and parchment and return to the oven to bake for 5 minutes longer. Cool slightly, then spread a thin layer of frangipane over the bottom of each tartlet shell. Bake until the frangipane is lightly golden, 8–10 minutes.

MEANWHILE, MAKE THE CRUMBLE. Put the flour, salt, and butter in a food processor and blend briefly until the mixture looks like fine crumbs. Add the sugar and ground almonds and pulse for a few seconds to mix. Don't overprocess: the mixture should be crumbly and uneven in texture.

SPREAD A LITTLE PLUM PURÉE in each tartlet shell. Arrange 5–6 poached plum segments in an overlapping circle on top, with the skins facing out.

SPRINKLE A LITTLE CRUMBLE onto the centre of each tart and dust lightly with icing sugar. Bake until the crumble topping is golden, about 5 minutes. Let the tarts cool.

TO SERVE, pipe a flower outline on each serving plate, using the melted chocolate. Fill with the plum sauce, using the back of a teaspoon to help spread the sauce. Place a plum tart in the centre. Serve with clotted cream or vanilla ice cream.

Raspberry compote with tarragon cream THESE LITTLE LIGHT CUSTARD

POTS ARE EASY TO PREPARE. MAKE THE RASPBERRY COMPOTE AND TARRAGON CREAM SEVERAL HOURS

IN ADVANCE AND KEEP THEM CHILLED, READY TO ASSEMBLE AND SERVE. *[Illustrated on page 103]*

Serves 6–8

RASPBERRY COMPOTE:
8 oz (250 g) raspberries
¹⁄₄ cup (50 mL) granulated sugar

TARRAGON CREAM:
Scant 1 cup (200 mL) whipping cream
Scant 1 cup (200 mL) whole milk
Scant ¹⁄₂ cup (100 mL) tarragon leaves, roughly chopped
7 tbsp (105 mL) granulated sugar
7 extra large egg yolks

FOR SERVING:
Unsweetened cocoa powder, for dusting

FOR THE RASPBERRY COMPOTE, put the raspberries and sugar in a non-stick pan and cook over high heat for a few minutes, shaking the pan, until the fruit has broken down and the juices are reduced and syrupy. Tip into a bowl and let cool completely.

SPOON A THIN LAYER of raspberry compote into 6 to 8 small serving glasses (or individual glass pots, as we do in the restaurant), reserving about 2 tbsp for serving. Cover the pots with plastic wrap and chill.

FOR THE TARRAGON CREAM, heat the cream, milk, and chopped tarragon in a saucepan with 1 tbsp (15 mL) sugar. As soon as the liquid starts to boil, remove the pan from the heat and set aside to infuse for 15–20 minutes.

BEAT THE EGG YOLKS AND THE REST OF THE SUGAR together in a large bowl until light and creamy, then pour in the tarragon-infused cream mixture, stirring until smooth.

POUR THE CREAMY MIXTURE into a large heavy-based saucepan and place over low heat. Stir with a wooden spoon until the custard is thick enough to lightly coat the back of the spoon. Pass the tarragon cream through a fine sieve into a clean bowl; discard the tarragon. Let cool, stirring occasionally to prevent a skin from forming on the surface. Cover with plastic wrap and chill for a few hours, or overnight, so the custard can firm up slightly.

TO SERVE, spoon the tarragon cream into the serving glasses to form a thick layer on the raspberry compote. Dust the surface with cocoa powder, then carefully drop a scant teaspoonful of the reserved raspberry compote on top. Serve immediately.

Pineapple ravioli with mango filling, berries, and mint sorbet

THIS FRUITY DESSERT IS WONDERFULLY REFRESHING, ESPECIALLY WHEN SERVED WITH A FRESH MINT SORBET, AS WE DO IN THE RESTAURANT. FOR A MORE INTENSE FLAVOUR WE FOLD REDUCED MANGO PURÉE THROUGH THE RAVIOLI FILLING, BUT THIS IS NOT ESSENTIAL. STEEP THE PINEAPPLE SLICES IN THE SYRUP OVERNIGHT AND PREPARE THE MINT SORBET 4–6 HOURS AHEAD. *[Illustrated on page 104]*

Serves 6–8

PINEAPPLE RAVIOLI :
Scant 1 cup (200 mL) stock syrup (see page 251)
2 tbsp (30 mL) light rum
Juice of ½ lemon
1 vanilla bean, split lengthwise and seeds removed (keep for the mango filling)
1 large, ripe pineapple

MINT SORBET:
1 cup (250 mL) lemon juice (from about 6 lemons)
1 cup (250 mL) stock syrup (see page 251)
Large bunch of mint, leaves only
½ cup (125 mL) crème de menthe

MANGO FILLING:
1 large mango
¼ cup (50 mL) crème fraîche
¼ cup (50 mL) mascarpone
Seeds from ½ vanilla bean
¼ cup (50 mL) mango purée
2–3 tbsp (30–45 mL) sifted icing sugar (optional)

FOR SERVING:
Scant 4 oz (100 g) mixed berries (such as blueberries, raspberries, and baby strawberries)
Candied orange peel (optional)
Few crystallized mint leaves (optional)

FOR THE PINEAPPLE RAVIOLI, pour the stock syrup and scant 1 cup (200 mL) water into a medium saucepan and add the rum, lemon juice, and vanilla bean. Bring to a boil and bubble for 5 minutes until reduced slightly, then transfer to a large bowl and let cool.

TO PREPARE THE PINEAPPLE, cut off the top and base, then stand the fruit upright on the board and slice away the skin, following the natural curve of the fruit. Prise out any remaining "eyes" with the tip of a sharp knife. Now turn the pineapple on its side and cut 16–24 very thin slices, using a long, serrated knife. Lay the pineapple slices in the cooled syrup as you cut them, insuring that each slice is well coated before adding another. Cover the bowl with plastic wrap and let macerate in the fridge overnight, so the pineapple slices soften.

TO MAKE THE MINT SORBET, put the lemon juice, stock syrup, mint, and 1½ cups (350 mL) water into a saucepan and bring to a boil. Boil for 2–3 minutes, then take off the heat and set aside to infuse and cool completely. Pour through a fine sieve into a bowl to strain out the mint leaves. Stir the crème de menthe into the infused syrup, then pour into an ice-cream maker and churn until almost firm. Transfer to a plastic container and freeze. (For the best texture, serve this sorbet the day it is made.)

FOR THE MANGO FILLING, peel the fruit and cut the flesh away from the pit, then chop into ¼-inch (5-mm) cubes. Mix the crème fraîche, mascarpone, and vanilla seeds together in a bowl, then stir in the mango purée. Fold in the chopped mango and sweeten with icing sugar to taste. Keep refrigerated.

WHEN READY TO SERVE, drain the pineapple slices, reserving the liquid. To thicken this if required, pour into a small pan and boil until reduced and syrupy, 5–7 minutes.

TO ASSEMBLE, pat each pineapple slice with paper towels, then place the smallest six slices on individual serving plates. Using a small ice-cream scoop, shape the mango filling into balls and place one on the centre of each pineapple base. Drape one or two larger pineapple slices over the top and press down the sides slightly to mould around the filling. Arrange the berries around the plates. If using, top each blueberry with a sliver of candied orange peel and each raspberry with a crystallized mint leaf. Drizzle a little pineapple syrup over the top and serve.

Pineapple and chili soup with fromage blanc foam

I LOVE THIS FRIVOLOUS DESSERT WITH ITS CONTRASTING LAYERS OF FLAVOURS—TANGY PINEAPPLE, LIGHT LEMONY FROMAGE BLANC, AND FLAVOUR BURSTS OF CHILI AND STARDUST CANDY. PREPARE THE PINEAPPLE SOUP AND THE CHILI SYRUP WELL IN ADVANCE. *[Illustrated on page 105]*

Serves 4–6

PINEAPPLE SOUP:
1 large, ripe pineapple
¼ cup (50 mL) granulated sugar, or to taste
⅓ cup (75 mL) Champagne or sparkling white wine
Splash of pineapple juice, to taste

CHILI SYRUP (OPTIONAL):
¼ cup (50 mL) stock syrup (see page 251)
Pinch of hot pepper flakes

FROMAGE BLANC FOAM:
Scant 4 oz (100 g) fromage blanc
½ cup (125 mL) whole milk
⅔ cup (150 mL) stock syrup (see page 251)
Juice of 2 lemons
2 sheets of leaf gelatin

FOR SERVING:
Few pinches of stardust candy (optional)
1 dried hot chili pepper, seeded and very finely chopped

TO PREPARE THE PINEAPPLE, cut off the top and base, then stand the fruit upright on the board and slice away the skin, following the natural curve of the fruit. Prise out any remaining "eyes" with the tip of a sharp knife. Cut into quarters lengthwise, remove the tough central core, and roughly chop the flesh. Toss the pineapple chunks with the sugar. Place a large skillet over high heat, add the pineapple, and toss for a few minutes until the chunks begin to soften and caramelize slightly.

TIP THE PINEAPPLE into a food processor or blender and blitz to a fine purée. Pass through a fine sieve into a bowl, pushing the pulp in the sieve with the back of a ladle to extract all the juice. Discard the pulp. Taste the strained juice and balance out the flavour with the Champagne and a splash of pineapple juice. Cover the bowl with plastic wrap and refrigerate.

FOR THE CHILI SYRUP, if using, bring the sugar syrup to a boil, add a pinch of pepper flakes, and remove from the heat. Let cool completely, then strain through a fine sieve and refrigerate.

FOR THE FROMAGE BLANC FOAM, beat the fromage blanc and milk together in a large bowl. Put the stock syrup and lemon juice in a saucepan, bring to a boil, and let bubble until slightly reduced, about 5 minutes.

MEANWHILE, SOAK THE GELATIN leaves in cold water to cover for a few minutes until softened. Take the lemon syrup off the heat. Drain the gelatin leaves and squeeze out excess water, then add to the hot lemon syrup, stirring to dissolve. Let cool slightly for about 5 minutes, then whisk into the fromage blanc mixture. Place the bowl over a larger bowl or pan filled with ice water. Whisk the mixture every now and then as it cools and starts to set. When it is softly set, cover the bowl with plastic wrap and refrigerate.

WHEN READY TO SERVE, half-fill four to six chilled tall glasses with the pineapple soup. If using chili syrup, add a tiny drizzle to each glass and drop in a large pinch of stardust candy, if you like.

WHISK THE FROMAGE BLANC FOAM with a balloon whisk or an electric mixer until light and airy. (In the restaurant we use a soda siphon to make and apply the foam, but this method works too.)

SPOON THE FOAM into the glasses and sprinkle a tiny pinch of dried chopped chili on top. Push a long, wide straw into each glass and serve.

Sablé breton with raspberries, vanilla cream, and vanilla ice cream

THESE LITTLE SHORTBREADS HAVE A LOVELY, BUTTERY FLAVOUR—THE PERFECT BASE FOR STRAWBERRIES AND VANILLA CREAM. MAKE THE SABLÉ DOUGH AHEAD AND FREEZE IT IF YOU LIKE—CUT INTO DISCS AND BAKE FROM FROZEN, ALLOWING AN EXTRA FEW MINUTES. THE DESSERT IS QUICK TO ASSEMBLE IF YOU MAKE THE VANILLA CREAM AND RASPBERRY BUTTER SAUCE IN ADVANCE, TOO.

[Illustrated on page 107]

Serves 10–12

SABLÉ BRETON:
Scant 8 oz (225 g) all-purpose flour (about 1⅔ cups/400 mL)
Pinch of fine sea salt
1 tbsp (15 mL) baking powder
⅔ cup (150 mL) salted butter, softened to room temperature, plus extra for brushing
¾ cup (175 mL) granulated sugar
4 extra large egg yolks, lightly beaten

VANILLA CREAM:
1 cup (250 mL) whole milk
½ vanilla bean, split lengthwise
¼ cup (50 mL) granulated sugar
3 large egg yolks
2½ tbsp (37 mL) cornstarch
⅓–½ cup (75–125 mL) whipping cream

RASPBERRY BUTTER SAUCE:
12 oz (350 g) raspberries
4 tbsp (60 mL) stock syrup (see page 251)
⅓ cup (75 mL) unsalted butter, diced

TO ASSEMBLE:
Melted bittersweet chocolate, for decoration
5 oz (150 g) raspberries
Icing sugar, for dusting
4 scoops of vanilla ice cream (see page 251)
Bittersweet chocolate rectangles (optional)
Handful of sugar-coated pistachios (optional)
Reduced stock syrup (see page 251), for drizzling

FOR THE SABLÉ BRETON, sift the flour, salt, and baking powder together and set aside. Using an electric mixer, beat the butter until it is light and creamy. Add the sugar and continue to beat, scraping the bowl as necessary, until the mixture is light and fluffy. Beat in the egg yolks, a little at a time, until fully incorporated. Now using a large rubber spatula, fold in the sifted dry ingredients, taking care to avoid overworking the dough.

SHAPE THE DOUGH into a thick log about 3 inches (8 cm) in diameter and wrap tightly in plastic wrap. Chill for a few hours until firm. (The sablé dough can also be frozen for up to a month.)

TO MAKE THE VANILLA CREAM, pour the milk into a saucepan. Scrape out the vanilla seeds and add these to the milk with the empty pod and 1 tbsp (15 mL) sugar. Slowly bring to a boil. Meanwhile, beat the remaining sugar and the egg yolks together in a large bowl until creamy. Beat in the cornstarch until the mixture is smooth. Just as the milk begins to boil, remove from the heat and gradually trickle onto the egg mixture, whisking constantly. When completely incorporated, pass through a fine sieve into a clean pan. Stir the mixture over low heat for 5 minutes or so, to cook the cornstarch and thicken the custard. Pass through a sieve into a large bowl. Let cool, stirring occasionally to prevent a skin from forming.

WHIP THE CREAM in another bowl to soft peaks, then fold into the cooled custard. Transfer to a large pastry bag and refrigerate.

PREHEAT THE OVEN to 350°F (180°C). Lightly butter 10–12 metal pastry rings about 3 inches (8 cm) in diameter, and place them on a large baking sheet; alternatively use a 12-hole muffin pan. Unwrap the sablé dough log and slice it into ⅝-inch (1.5-cm) discs. Put a disc in each pastry ring and bake until pale golden in colour, 8–10 minutes. Let cool in the metal rings for a few minutes, then transfer to a wire rack to cool completely. Store in an airtight container if not serving immediately.

FOR THE RASPBERRY BUTTER SAUCE, blend the raspberries and stock syrup together in a blender, then rub the purée through a fine sieve into a small pan. Bring the raspberry purée to a boil and bubble until reduced by about one-third, to scant 1 cup (200 mL). Turn down the heat and slowly whisk in the butter to make a smooth, glossy sauce. Pour into a bowl and let cool completely.

TO ASSEMBLE, spoon some raspberry sauce onto each serving plate and pipe some lines of melted chocolate across the plates. Place a sablé breton base next to the sauce and pipe a generous mound of vanilla cream in the centre.

ARRANGE THE RASPBERRIES around the vanilla cream and dust lightly with icing sugar. Place a scoop of vanilla ice cream next to the raspberry sablé breton. If using, top the vanilla creams with chocolate rectangles and pipe a little blob of vanilla cream on top, then finish with a sugar-coated pistachio. Drizzle each plate with a few drops of reduced stock syrup and scatter a few sugar-coated pistachios around. Serve immediately.

Tiramisu with coffee granita

THIS IS MY TWIST ON A CLASSIC TIRAMISU—A LIGHT COFFEE CREAM SITS ATOP AN ESPRESSO GRANITA AND MASCARPONE SORBET IN A MARTINI GLASS. IN THE RESTAURANT, WE USE A SODA SIPHON TO APPLY THE TIRAMISU CREAM, WHICH CREATES A FROTHY FOAM, BUT THIS SIMPLIFIED VERSION TASTES JUST AS GOOD. *[Illustrated on page 108]*

Serves 6–8

ESPRESSO GRANITA:
¾ cup (175 mL) granulated sugar
6 shots (or 1 cup + 2 tbsp/270 mL) single espresso, cooled

MASCARPONE SORBET:
¼ cup (50 mL) granulated sugar
Juice of ½ lemon
1 heaped tbsp (20 mL) liquid glucose (or light corn syrup)
1 lb (500 g) mascarpone

TIRAMISU:
1 sheet of leaf gelatin
2 shots (or 6 tbsp/90 mL) hot double espresso
¼ cup (50 mL) granulated sugar
3 extra large egg yolks
⅔ cup (150 mL) mascarpone
¼ cup (50 mL) whole milk
⅓ cup (75 mL) whipping cream

FOR SERVING:
Unsweetened cocoa powder, for dusting
Cotton candy (optional)

FIRST, MAKE THE GRANITA. Put the sugar and 1 cup (250 mL) water into a saucepan and stir over low heat until the sugar has dissolved. Increase the heat and bring to a boil. Let the syrup boil for 3 minutes, then remove from the heat. Pour in the espresso and cool completely. Transfer to a shallow, rigid container and freeze until partially frozen, 2–3 hours.

USE A FORK TO BREAK UP the semi-frozen granita, stirring the crystallized flakes around the edges into the liquid centre, then return the granita to the freezer. Continue freezing, stirring the mixture 2 or 3 times more during the process. The completely frozen granita will have a granular texture.

FOR THE MASCARPONE SORBET, put the sugar, lemon juice, liquid glucose, and 7 tbsp (105 mL) water into a saucepan. Stir over low heat until the sugar has dissolved, then increase the heat and boil the syrup for a few minutes. Set aside to cool completely.

BEAT THE MASCARPONE in a large bowl to loosen it slightly. Gradually stir in the cooled syrup until it is evenly incorporated. Transfer to an ice-cream machine and churn until almost firm. Scrape the ice cream into a plastic container and freeze until firm.

TO MAKE THE TIRAMISU, soak the gelatin leaf in cold water to cover for a few minutes until soft. Drain and squeeze out excess water, then add to the piping hot espresso and stir until dissolved. Set aside to cool.

MEANWHILE, place the sugar and egg yolks in a large heatproof bowl and beat lightly to mix. Set the bowl over a pan of barely simmering water and beat the yolks and sugar together, using a portable electric mixer. Keep beating until the sabayon almost triples in volume and becomes thick and pale. When you lift the beaters out, the sabayon should leave a ribbon trail on the surface that lasts for 10 minutes.

FOLD THE COOLED COFFEE mixture into the sabayon very carefully. Beat the mascarpone, milk, and cream together in another bowl, then fold into the coffee sabayon base. Cover the bowl with plastic wrap and refrigerate.

LET THE MASCARPONE SORBET soften at room temperature for about 5 minutes before serving.

TO SERVE, place a heaped tablespoonful of espresso granita in a cocktail glass and add a scoop of mascarpone sorbet. Spoon the tiramisu cream on top and dust with a little cocoa powder. Decorate each serving with a little cotton candy, if you like. Serve at once.

Raspberry, lemon, and basil millefeuille with milk ice cream

WAVY CHOCOLATE TUILES ARE LAYERED WITH ALTERNATE BANDS OF RASPBERRY AND LEMON MOUSSE FOR A STUNNING DESSERT. MAKE THE TUILES AND MILK ICE CREAM WELL IN ADVANCE. YOU CAN ALSO PREPARE THE STABLE ITALIAN MERINGUE FOR THE MOUSSES A FEW HOURS AHEAD. ASSEMBLE THE MILLEFEUILLES JUST BEFORE SERVING TO KEEP THE TUILES CRISP. *[Illustrated on page 112]*

Serves 6–8

MILK ICE CREAM:
4 cups (1 L) whole milk
4 tbsp (60 mL) condensed milk
1 tsp (5 mL) liquid glucose (or light corn syrup)

CHOCOLATE TUILES:
4 tbsp (60 mL) whole milk
6 tbsp (90 mL) dark brown sugar (preferably muscovado sugar)
2/3 cup (150 mL) icing sugar
1 cup (250 mL) all-purpose flour
2½ tbsp (37 mL) unsweetened cocoa powder
2 oz (55 g) egg whites (from about 2 extra large eggs)

ITALIAN MERINGUE:
½ cup (125 mL) granulated sugar
1 tsp (5 mL) liquid glucose (or light corn syrup)
2 extra large egg whites

LEMON AND BASIL MOUSSE:
2 sheets of leaf gelatin
¼ cup (50 mL) granulated sugar
2/3 cup (150 mL) lemon juice (from about 4 lemons)
10 large basil leaves, finely chopped

RASPBERRY MOUSSE:
2 sheets of leaf gelatin
1¼ lb (550 g) raspberries

TO FINISH THE MOUSSES:
1¾ cups (400 mL) whipping cream

FOR SERVING:
Melted bittersweet chocolate, for drizzling
Crushed nougatine (see page 214), optional
Reduced stock syrup (see page 251), optional
Handful of raspberries
Candied lime rind (optional)

FIRST, MAKE THE MILK ICE CREAM. Boil the milk in a wide pan until it has reduced by two-thirds to about 1½ cups (375 mL). Mix the condensed milk and liquid glucose in a large bowl. Pour in the reduced milk and stir well. Cool the mixture quickly by standing the bowl over another bowl of ice water. Then pour into an ice-cream machine and churn until almost firm. Transfer to a shallow container and freeze.

TO MAKE THE CHOCOLATE TUILES, put the milk and brown sugar in a pan and stir over low heat until the sugar has dissolved. Set aside to cool. Sift the icing sugar, flour, and cocoa together into a large bowl. Stir in the cooled milk, a little at a time to avoid lumps forming. Add the egg whites and mix well.

PREHEAT THE OVEN to 350°F (180°C). Line a large, rimless baking sheet with a silicone baking mat. Use a metal spatula to smooth out a thin layer of the tuile batter on the mat, then use the edge of the spatula to mark out 5- by 1¼-inch (12- by 3-cm) rectangles. Bake until the chocolate tuiles are fairly firm around the edges, 6–7 minutes. Meanwhile, lay two large, thick-handled wooden spoons side-by-side on a board. Leave the tuiles for a few seconds, then lift off the mat with the spatula and drape over the spoon handles. The tuiles will set in a wave fashion and become crisp on cooling. Repeat to make at least 24 tuiles. When cool, store in an airtight container.

TO MAKE THE ITALIAN MERINGUE, put the sugar, 2–3 tbsp (15–30 mL) water, and liquid glucose in a saucepan and stir over low heat until the syrup is clear. Increase the heat and boil until it reaches 250°F (120°C) on a candy thermometer, 5–7 minutes. Meanwhile, beat the egg whites in an electric mixer to soft peaks. Slowly trickle the hot syrup onto the egg whites, beating all the time. Keep beating until the meringue is firm, white, and glossy, and the bowl no longer feels hot, about 5 minutes. Set aside.

TO MAKE THE LEMON MOUSSE, soak the gelatin in cold water to cover for a few minutes to soften. Meanwhile, put the sugar and lemon juice in a small saucepan and stir over low heat until dissolved. Bring to a boil, then pour into a large bowl. Drain the gelatin, squeeze out excess water, and add to the hot lemon syrup, stirring to dissolve. Let cool, stirring occasionally.

FOR THE RASPBERRY MOUSSE, soak the gelatin in cold water to soften. Put about four-fifths of the raspberries in a non-stick pan and stir over high heat until softened and starting to break up. Pass through a fine sieve set over a large bowl to make a purée, pressing to extract all the raspberry juice. Drain the gelatin, squeeze out excess liquid, and add to the raspberry purée, stirring to dissolve. (If the purée has cooled, reheat to just below a boil.) Let cool, stirring occasionally.

DIVIDE THE ITALIAN MERINGUE in half. Fold one portion into the lemon mousse mixture and the other half into the raspberry mousse mixture, in each case until just beginning to set. In another bowl, whip the cream to firm peaks, then fold half into each mousse. Fold the chopped basil into the lemon mousse. Finely chop the remaining raspberries and fold into the raspberry mousse. Spoon each mousse into a large pastry bag fitted with a large plain tip and chill for 2–3 hours.

TO ASSEMBLE THE MILLEFEUILLE, place a chocolate tuile on a clean surface. Pipe a band of lemon mousse along the length of the tuile, then pipe a band of raspberry mousse alongside. Put another chocolate tuile on top. Repeat piping the mousse bands, but this time switching the order so that you end up with alternating colours. Top with a third chocolate tuile. Repeat to assemble a millefeuille for each serving.

TO SERVE, pipe decorative patterns of melted chocolate on each plate, if you like. Put two little dollops of mousse on one side of the plate and set a millefeuille on top. Place a neat teaspoon of crushed nougatine on the side, if using. Top with a scoop of milk ice cream. Drizzle some melted chocolate over the ice cream and finish each plate with dots of reduced stock syrup, if using. Add a little pile of raspberries, topped with candied lime rind, if wished. Serve immediately.

Palet d'or with chocolate and hazelnut ice cream and passion fruit cream

THIS IS A RICH, GLOSSY CHOCOLATE GANACHE, MADE ALL THE MORE INTERESTING BY SERVING WITH A CHOCOLATE AND HAZELNUT ICE CREAM, TANGY PASSION FRUIT CREAM, AND A SURPRISING GIN JELLY. YOU WILL NEED TO MAKE THE GANACHE AND ASSEMBLE THE DESSERT JUST BEFORE SERVING, BUT ALL THE OTHER COMPONENTS CAN BE MADE IN ADVANCE. *[Illustrated on page 114]*

Serves 6–8

CHOCOLATE AND HAZELNUT ICE CREAM:
2¼ cups (550 mL) whole milk
2 tbsp (30 mL) liquid glucose (or light corn syrup)
8 extra large egg yolks
2 tbsp (30 mL) granulated sugar
7 oz (200 g) gianduja paste (chocolate and hazelnut paste)

GIN GELÉE:
3 sheets of leaf gelatin
1 cup (250 mL) gin

SPONGE CAKE:
½ cup + 1 tbsp (140 mL) unsalted butter, softened to room temperature
1 cup (250 mL) icing sugar
6 extra large eggs, separated (yolks lightly beaten)
4 oz (125 g) bittersweet chocolate, melted and cooled
1 cup (250 mL) superfine sugar
4¼ oz (130 g) all-purpose flour (about scant 1 cup/250 mL), sifted

CHOCOLATE TUILES:
2 egg whites
½ cup (125 mL) superfine sugar
6 tbsp (90 mL) all-purpose flour
Scant 1 tsp (scant 5 mL) unsweetened cocoa powder
¼ cup (50 mL) unsalted butter, melted and cooled

PASSION FRUIT CREAM:
½ cup (125 mL) whipping cream
¼ cup (50 mL) granulated sugar
Juice from 2 passion fruit, strained

CHOCOLATE GANACHE:
⅔ cup (150 mL) whipping cream
6 oz (175 g) baking chocolate (about 66% cocoa solids), chopped
1½ tbsp (25 mL) liquid glucose (or light corn syrup)
2 tbsp (30 mL) unsalted butter

FOR SERVING (OPTIONAL):
Finely crushed cocoa nibs, for sprinkling

FIRST, MAKE THE ICE CREAM. Put the milk and liquid glucose into a saucepan and stir over low heat until the glucose has melted. Slowly bring to a boil. Meanwhile, beat the egg yolks and sugar in a bowl, then stir in the chocolate and hazelnut paste; the mixture will be quite thick. As soon as the milk starts to boil, take off the heat and slowly pour onto the egg mixture, stirring until smooth.

PASS THROUGH A FINE SIEVE into a clean pan. Stir over low heat until the custard thickens enough to lightly coat the back of the spoon. Strain through a fine sieve into a bowl. Cool, stirring now and then to prevent a skin from forming. Transfer to an ice-cream machine and churn until almost firm. Scoop into a shallow container and freeze until firm.

FOR THE GIN GELÉE, soak the gelatin in cold water to cover for a few minutes to soften. Warm the gin in a small pan but don't let it boil; take off the heat. Drain the gelatin and squeeze out excess water, then add to the gin, stirring until dissolved. Pour into a shallow container and cool completely. Cover and chill for a few hours, or overnight, to set.

FOR THE CAKE, preheat the oven to 325°F (160°C). Line a loose-bottomed 12-inch (30-cm) square cake pan with parchment paper. Beat the butter and icing sugar together in a large bowl until pale and creamy. Gradually beat in the egg yolks, then fold in the chocolate.

BEAT THE EGG WHITES in a clean, dry bowl to firm peaks, using an electric mixer. Slowly beat in the superfine sugar, a tablespoonful at a time, to make a firm meringue. Carefully fold the flour into the chocolate batter, then fold in the meringue. Spread the batter in the cake pan. Bake until the cake feels springy when lightly pressed and a skewer inserted into the centre comes out clean, 50–60 minutes. Let cool in the pan.

MEANWHILE, MAKE THE TUILES. Line a rimless baking sheet with a silicone baking mat. Put the egg whites and sugar in a bowl and lightly beat with a fork. Sift in the flour with the cocoa powder and stir to mix well. Add the butter and stir until evenly blended.

USING A METAL SPATULA, spread a few thin strips of the tuile mixture on the mat. Bake until brown at the edges, with a matt appearance, 7–8 minutes. Let cool for a minute or two. Just before they set, while still pliable, lift each tuile with the spatula and twist to resemble a pair of wings. Let cool and set; they will become crisp and brittle. Repeat to make more tuiles until you have used up the batter. Store in an airtight container.

FOR THE PASSION FRUIT CREAM, put the cream and sugar in a small saucepan and stir over low heat until the sugar has dissolved. Increase the heat and bubble for 3 minutes.

LOWER THE HEAT, stir in the passion fruit juice, and simmer until it has the consistency of a thick but still pourable cream. Let cool.

AN HOUR BEFORE SERVING, put all the ingredients for the ganache into a double boiler (or heatproof bowl set over a pan of gently simmering water). Stir until the mixture is smooth and shiny. Keep warm while assembling the dessert.

TRIM THE SIDES and top of the cake to even them, then cut it into 12 or 16 neat squares. Spread a layer of ganache over one square, then put another on top, with the flat side facing up. Repeat with the remaining cake squares. Place the cake sandwiches on a wire rack set over a rimmed baking sheet.

POUR A LAYER OF GANACHE over each cake sandwich to cover, letting the excess drip down the sides. Use a metal spatula to smooth the ganache over the sides. Leave for 30–40 minutes to let the ganache firm up.

TO PLATE, spoon the passion fruit cream decoratively onto the serving plates. Using a clean metal spatula, carefully lift a ganache-covered cake onto each plate. Put a spoonful of gin gelée alongside. If using, sprinkle a little crushed cocoa nib on the plates. Top each palet d'or with a chocolate tuile and a neat scoop of chocolate and hazelnut ice cream. Serve immediately.

Slow-baked quince with crème catalan, Pedro Ximenez gelée, and acacia honey granita

THIS SPANISH-INSPIRED DESSERT COMBINES SOME OF MY FAVOURITE FLAVOURS—AROMATIC SHERRY, SWEET QUINCE, AND CREAMY CUSTARD. PREPARE ALL THE ELEMENTS FOR THIS DESSERT WELL AHEAD, READY TO ASSEMBLE JUST BEFORE SERVING. SPREAD ANY LEFTOVER QUINCE PURÉE ON WALNUT BREAD AND SERVE WITH MANCHEGO CHEESE. *[Illustrated on page 115]*

Serves about 8

QUINCE PURÉE:
2 large quinces, cleaned
1 cup + 2 tbsp (280 mL) granulated sugar
2 vanilla beans, split lengthwise

ACACIA HONEY GRANITA:
1/2 cup (125 mL) acacia honey
1 1/2 sheets of leaf gelatin

PEDRO XIMENEZ JELLY:
1 1/2 cups (375 mL) Pedro Ximenez sherry
3 sheets of leaf gelatin

CRÈME CATALAN:
2 cups (500 mL) whipping cream
1/3 cup (75 mL) whole milk
1/2 vanilla bean, split lengthwise
1/3 cup (75 mL) granulated sugar
2 extra large egg yolks

MINT CUSTARD:
1 cup (250 mL) whole milk
1 cup (250 mL) whipping cream
Small bunch of mint (about 6 sprigs), leaves only
1/3 cup (75 mL) granulated sugar
6 extra large egg yolks

FOR SERVING:
8–10 good-quality madeleines (optional)
16–20 thin tuiles sandwiched in pairs with quince purée (optional)

FIRST, MAKE THE QUINCE PURÉE. Preheat the oven to 275°F (140°C). Peel the quinces, then cut into quarters and remove the core. Roughly chop the flesh into small cubes and place in a wide stovetop-to-oven pan with the sugar. Pour in enough water to cover and stir over low heat until the sugar has dissolved. Scrape out the vanilla seeds and add to the pan with the empty pods. Increase the heat and bring the syrup to a boil. Cover the pan with a piece of foil and place in the oven.

BAKE UNTIL THE QUINCE is very soft, about 3 hours. While still hot, drain the quince, reserving the syrup, and put into a food processor or blender with a little of the syrup. Blend to a smooth purée. If too thick, blend in a little more of the reserved syrup. Let cool completely, then refrigerate.

NEXT, MAKE THE GRANITA. Put the honey and 2½ cups (625 mL) water in a saucepan and bring to a boil, stirring once or twice. Soak the gelatin leaves in cold water for a few minutes to soften. Boil the honey syrup until it begins to foam, then strain through a fine sieve into a wide bowl. Drain the gelatin leaves, squeeze out excess water, and add to the hot syrup, stirring until the gelatin dissolves. Let cool completely, stirring every once in a while, then pour the mixture into a shallow container. Cover and freeze until partially frozen, about 2 hours.

USE A FORK TO STIR the ice crystals into the still liquid centre. Freeze for 1–2 hours longer, then beat the mixture again and return to the freezer. Beat the mixture twice more during freezing to achieve a granular texture.

FOR THE JELLY, pour the sherry into a small pan and place over low heat. Meanwhile, soak the gelatin leaves in cold water for a few minutes to soften. When the sherry is hot enough for you to feel the heat rising from the pan (but not boiling), remove from the heat. Drain the gelatin leaves and squeeze out excess water, then add to the sherry and gently swirl the pan until the gelatin has dissolved. Let cool completely.

SPOON A THIN LAYER of quince purée into individual serving glasses. Carefully pour a layer of sherry jelly over the purée, using a teaspoon to guide the liquid in if you find it easier. Chill for a few hours, or overnight, until the jelly is softly set.

TO MAKE THE CRÈME CATALAN, pour the cream and milk into a heavy-based saucepan. Scrape the vanilla seeds into the pan and add the pod, too. Slowly bring to a boil. Meanwhile, beat the sugar and egg yolks together in a large bowl. When the creamy milk begins to bubble up the side of the pan, take off the heat. Slowly pour onto the sugar and yolks, whisking as you do so. Strain the mixture through a fine sieve into a clean pan.

STIR WITH A WOODEN SPOON over low heat until the mixture thickens into a light custard: It should coat the back of the spoon and leave an impression when you draw a finger down the spoon. Remove from the heat and strain through a fine sieve into a wide bowl. Let cool, stirring the custard occasionally to prevent a skin from forming. Cover and keep in the fridge until required.

FOR THE MINT CUSTARD, bring the milk and cream to a boil in a heavy-based saucepan, then immediately remove from the heat and add the mint leaves. Let cool and infuse for about 30 minutes. Beat the sugar and egg yolks together in a bowl. Strain the mint-infused cream onto the mixture, then pour into a clean pan. Stir over low heat until it thickens into a light custard (as for the crème catalan, left and above). Strain the custard through a fine sieve into a wide bowl and let cool completely, stirring occasionally to prevent a skin from forming. Pour the custard into a pitcher for serving.

TO ASSEMBLE, whisk the crème catalan to lighten it. Spoon a layer over the sherry jelly in each glass. Stand the glasses on serving plates. Top with a neat quenelle of acacia honey granita. If you like, serve a madeleine and a quince tuile alongside. Bring the desserts to the table and drizzle a little mint custard on top of the crème catalan as you serve.

Chocolate parfait with passion fruit and guava coulis IN THE

RESTAURANT WE USE GIANDUJA PASTE TO MAKE THESE PARFAITS. IT LENDS A LOVELY RICH FLAVOUR, BUT AS IT IS HARD TO FIND I HAVE USED DARK CHOCOLATE HERE INSTEAD. SIMILARLY, WE USE GUAVA AND PASSION FRUIT PURÉES PREPARED FOR RESTAURANTS. THE COULIS LENDS AN EQUALLY GOOD FLAVOUR, ALTHOUGH IT WILL NOT HAVE QUITE THE SAME INTENSITY OF COLOUR. *[Illustrated on page 118]*

Serves 10–12

CHOCOLATE PARFAIT:
¾ cup (175 mL) granulated sugar
8 extra large egg yolks
1½ cups (375mL) whipping cream
2 tbsp (30 mL) milk
5 oz (150 g) bittersweet chocolate, melted and cooled
7 tbsp (105 mL) vodka

PASSION FRUIT AND GUAVA COULIS:
2 cups (500 mL) guava juice
Juice from 8 ripe passion fruit, strained
3 tbsp (45 mL) stock syrup (see page 251)
2 tsp (10 mL) arrowroot

FOR SERVING:
Melted bittersweet chocolate, for piping
Unsweetened cocoa powder, for dusting (optional)

FOR THE PARFAIT, first prepare a pâte à bombe: Dissolve the sugar in scant ½ cup (100 mL) water in a heavy-based saucepan over low heat, then increase the heat to high and bring the syrup to a boil. Meanwhile, beat the egg yolks in an electric mixer until pale and creamy. Boil the syrup until it registers 250°F (120°C) on a candy thermometer. With the mixer on the highest speed, slowly trickle the hot syrup onto the egg yolks. Keep beating until the mixture is thick and smooth and has substantially increased in volume. Beat until the bowl no longer feels hot, then set aside to cool.

IN ANOTHER BOWL, whip the cream with the milk to soft peaks using an electric mixer. Fold the melted chocolate into the pâte à bombe, then fold in the whipped cream and, finally, the vodka. Spoon the parfait into ⅔-cup (150-mL) individual moulds and cover with plastic wrap. Freeze the parfait for a few hours, or overnight, until firm.

FOR THE COULIS, boil the guava juice until reduced to scant 1 cup (200 mL). Add the passion fruit juice and stock syrup. Mix the arrowroot with 1 tsp (5 mL) water, then add to the pan. Stir over medium-low heat until the mixture is smooth and has thickened to a shiny, syrupy sauce. Pass through a fine sieve into a bowl and let cool. When cold, transfer the coulis to a plastic squeezy bottle and refrigerate.

TO SERVE, pipe lines of melted chocolate on each chilled serving plate to create a decorative square (as shown). Fill the squares with the passion fruit and guava coulis, using the back of a teaspoon to help spread the coulis, if necessary. Set aside.

UNMOULD THE PARFAITS one at a time: Dip the base of the mould into a bowl of hot water for a few seconds, then run a thin knife along the edges of the parfait to loosen it. Unmould it onto a board or large plate and dust with cocoa powder, if using. (At the restaurant, we use a special spray gun to dust the parfaits with cocoa powder. You may not be able to achieve such an even result without one, but that won't affect the taste.) Use a metal spatula to transfer the parfait to a decorated plate. Keep in the fridge while you assemble the rest of the plates. Serve at once.

Bitter chocolate mousse with coffee granita and light ginger cream

THIS GORGEOUS DESSERT IS SO POPULAR WITH OUR CUSTOMERS, IT IS FAST BECOMING A CLASSIC. WE OFTEN VARY THE TYPE OF MOUSSE IN THE CHOCOLATE CYLINDER—ALTERNATING BETWEEN GIANDUJA, PRALINE, AND DARK CHOCCLATE. YOU WILL NEED TO PREPARE THE DIFFERENT ELEMENTS OF THIS DESSERT IN ADVANCE, READY TO ASSEMBLE JUST BEFORE SERVING. *[Illustrated on page 119]*

Serves 6

CHOCOLATE CYLINDER:
10 oz (300 g) dark couverture chocolate (see page 252), chopped

CARAMELIZED RICE CRISPIES:
¼ cup (50 mL) granulated sugar
1 cup (250 mL) rice crispies

LIGHT GINGER FOAM:
⅓ cup (75 mL) whipping cream
¾ cup (175 mL) whole milk
2½ tbsp (37 mL) granulated sugar
½ oz (15 g) gingerroot, peeled and grated
¾ sheet of leaf gelatin

BITTER CHOCOLATE MOUSSE:
4 oz (125 g) bittersweet chocolate (minimum 75% cocoa solids), broken into small pieces
3 tbsp (45 mL) butter
3 egg yolks
½ cup (125 mL) granulated sugar
½ cup (125 mL) whipping cream
3 oz (90 g) egg whites (from about 2 extra large eggs)

FOR SERVING:
Melted bittersweet chocolate, for decorating
6 brownie squares (see page 241)
6 small spoonfuls espresso granita (see page 228)
6 pieces of chocolate sticks (optional)
6 small pieces of edible gold leaf (optional)
6 scoops of milk ice cream (see page 230)

FOR THE CHOCOLATE CYLINDERS, you first need to temper the chocolate. For this, you will need a digital probe thermometer to assess the temperature of the chocolate. Set aside 2 oz (60 g) of the chopped couverture. Place the rest in a glass mixing bowl and microwave on high for 30 seconds at a time until most of the chocolate has melted. Give it a stir each time and check the temperature—you want it to reach about 115°F (45°C).

ADD THE REMAINING CHOCOLATE and stir constantly. Let the temperature of the combined chocolate fall to 80°F (27°C), then microwave in 5–10-second bursts until the temperature climbs up to 88°F (31°C). To test if the chocolate is tempered, dip in the tip of a thin metal spatula, tap off any excess, and let set for 5 minutes. It should harden in a few minutes and have a shiny gloss. If not, repeat the tempering process. (Note: Do not overheat the chocolate as it cannot be tempered again once it has seized.)

ONCE TEMPERED, stand the bowl of chocolate in a larger bowl of lukewarm water to maintain the temperature at about 88°F (31°C).

TO MAKE THE CYLINDERS, you will need seven 2¼-inch (6-cm) round metal cutters, a large sheet of acetate, and six acetate rectangles, each 3 by 8 inches (8 by 20 cm). Using a small metal spatula, spread a ¹⁄₁₆-inch (2-mm) layer of tempered chocolate over each acetate rectangle and let it set a little. When the chocolate begins to firm up, carefully curve the acetate into a metal cutter so that it forms a cylinder. If you wish, tape the overlapping ends of the acetate to secure the shape of the cylinder. Using the back of a teaspoon, smooth a little more chocolate over the area where the ends of the acetate meet, to seal the cylinder. Repeat to make six cylinders (or more, to allow for possible breakages during the final assembly).

TO MAKE THE ROUND TOPS, spread a layer of tempered chocolate on the large sheet of acetate, then leave to set a little. As the chocolate begins to firm up, use the seventh metal cutter to press down and outline 6 circles. (You might like to use any remaining tempered chocolate to make extra tops, to allow for possible breakages.) Let the chocolate cylinders and tops set in a cool part of the kitchen.

TO MAKE THE CARAMELIZED RICE CRISPIES, line a rimmed baking sheet with a silicone baking mat, or lightly oil the sheet. Set aside. Scatter the sugar evenly in a heavy-based pan and place over high heat. Let the sugar melt and cook to a golden caramel. Remove the pan from the heat, add the rice crispies, and toss to coat, then immediately tip onto the baking sheet. Tilt the sheet to spread out the mixture and set aside to cool; the caramel will firm up and become brittle when cooled. Break the caramelized rice crispies into smaller pieces, then chop finely. Store in an airtight container until ready to use.

FOR THE GINGER FOAM, put the cream, milk, and sugar into a saucepan and bring to a boil. Remove from the heat, add the grated ginger, and set aside to infuse for 5 minutes. Meanwhile, soak the gelatin in cold water to cover for a few minutes to soften. Strain the infused cream through a fine sieve into a bowl and discard the ginger. Drain the gelatin and squeeze out excess water, then add to the warm cream and stir until dissolved. Chill the mixture for a few hours until it has partially set.

BEAT THE GINGER MIXTURE, using an electric mixer, until it is light and foamy, about 5 minutes. Return to the fridge and chill until set, 1–2 hours.

[continued on the next page]

FOR THE CHOCOLATE MOUSSE, melt the chocolate and butter together in a heatproof bowl set over a pan of barely simmering water. Cool slightly, stirring the mixture every once in a while.

NEXT, MAKE A PÂTE À BOMBE with the egg yolks and sugar: dissolve the sugar in 1/3 cup (75 mL) water in a heavy-based saucepan over low heat, then increase the heat to high and bring the syrup to a boil. Meanwhile, beat the egg yolks in an electric mixer until pale and creamy. Boil the syrup until it registers 250°F (120°C) on a candy thermometer. With the mixer on the highest speed, slowly trickle the hot syrup onto the egg yolks. Keep on beating until the mixture is thick and smooth and has substantially increased in volume. Beat until the bowl no longer feels hot, then set aside to cool to room temperature.

WHIP THE CREAM TO SOFT PEAKS. In another clean, dry bowl, beat the egg whites to soft peaks. Fold the chocolate mixture into the pâte à bombe, then fold in the whipped cream and, finally, the beaten egg whites.

JUST BEFORE SERVING, whisk up the ginger foam again until it is thick and creamy, then transfer to a pastry bag fitted with a large plain tip.

TO ASSEMBLE, pipe decorative chocolate lines on 6 serving plates. Cut the brownie squares horizontally to get slices about 1/8 inch (3 mm) thick. Using a round metal cutter slightly smaller than the chocolate cylinders, cut out discs from each brownie slice. Place a brownie disc on a serving plate. Carefully position a chocolate cylinder over the brownie disc. Cut off any tape with a knife and slowly and carefully unravel the acetate, gently pulling it away from the chocolate cylinder.

PIPE IN THE BITTER CHOCOLATE mousse to half-fill the cylinder. Sprinkle a little caramelized rice crispie on top, then add a spoonful of espresso granita. Pipe the ginger cream on top to come up slightly above the edge of the cylinder. Carefully remove a round chocolate disc from the acetate. If using, attach a chocolate stick and a small piece of gold leaf to the disc, using a bit of melted chocolate as glue. Set on top of the ginger foam. Put a scoop of milk ice cream on a little bed of caramelized rice crispie on the side of the plate and drizzle a little melted chocolate over this, if you like. Serve at once.

Apple parfait with honeycomb, bitter chocolate, and champagne foam

THIS IS AN IMPRESSIVE DESSERT, THOUGH RATHER TIME-CONSUMING TO PREPARE AT HOME. YOU COULD SIMPLIFY THE RECIPE BY OMITTING THE HONEYCOMB TUILES, MILK ICE CREAM, AND CHOCOLATE SPIRALS. YOU WILL HAVE EXTRA BROWNIES TO SERVE ON THE SIDE, OR THE FOLLOWING DAY. *[Illustrated on page 109]*

Serves 8

BROWNIE:
1 cup (250 mL) all-purpose flour
2/3 cup (150 mL) unsweetened
   cocoa powder
2/3 cup (150 mL) unsalted butter, softened
   to room temperature
1 1/2 cups (375 mL) granulated sugar
4 extra large eggs, lightly beaten
4 oz (125 g) bittersweet chocolate, chopped

APPLE GRANITA:
4 Granny Smith apples
Juice of 1 lemon
1 cup (250 mL) granulated sugar
1/4 cup (50 mL) liquid glucose (or
   light corn syrup)

APPLE PARFAIT:
2 3/4 oz (80 g) egg yolks (from
   about 4 extra large eggs)
1/2 cup (125 mL) granulated sugar
3 Granny Smith apples
Squeeze of lemon juice
1 3/4 cups (400 mL) apple cider
3 1/2 sheets of leaf gelatin
2/3 cup (150 mL) whipping cream
7 tbsp (105 mL) apple Bacardi
   (or clear rum)

HONEYCOMB TUILES:
3/4 cup (175 mL) granulated sugar
3 tbsp (45 mL) liquid glucose (or
   light corn syrup)
1/4 cup (50 mL) clear honey
2 tbsp (30 mL) baking soda

CHAMPAGNE FOAM:
1/4 cup (50 mL) granulated sugar
1/4 cup (50 mL) whole milk
1 sheet of leaf gelatin
1 cup (250 mL) Champagne
1/2 cup (125 mL) whipping cream

FOR SERVING:
Melted bittersweet chocolate,
   for decorating
Lightly toasted shredded coconut,
   for sprinkling (optional)
8 scoops of milk ice cream (see page 230)
Chocolate spirals, for decorating (optional)
Reduced apple syrup, for drizzling
   (optional)

[continued overleaf]

FIRST, MAKE THE BROWNIE. Preheat the oven to 325°F (160°C). Line an 8-inch (20-cm) square cake pan with parchment paper. Sift together the flour and cocoa powder. Put the butter and sugar in a large bowl and beat with an electric mixer until pale and fluffy. Gradually mix in the beaten eggs, a little at a time. Carefully fold in the sifted flour mixture followed by the chopped chocolate. Spread the batter in the prepared pan and bake until the brownie has set around the edges and feels fairly firm in the centre, 25–35 minutes. Unlike a conventional brownie, it should be more set in the middle so that it can be sliced horizontally into thin squares or rectangles.

LET THE BROWNIE COOL in the pan for 10 minutes, then transfer to a wire rack and let cool completely.

NEXT, MAKE THE APPLE GRANITA. Leaving the skins on, quarter and core the apples and immediately toss with the lemon juice. Place the apples in a single layer in plastic containers and freeze for 1 hour, to chill thoroughly and help intensify the colour.

MEANWHILE, dissolve the sugar in 1³/₄ cups (425 mL) water in a heavy-based pan over low heat. When the syrup is clear, increase the heat and bring to a boil. Boil until slightly reduced, about 5 minutes. Let cool completely, then stir in the liquid glucose.

REMOVE THE APPLES from the freezer and chop them roughly. Put them in a food processor with one-third of the sugar syrup and blitz until finely puréed, stopping to scrape down the sides of the processor once or twice. Mix with the rest of the syrup, then pass the mixture through a fine sieve into a large bowl. Rub the pulp in the sieve with the back of a ladle to extract all the juice.

POUR THE APPLE PURÉE into a shallow plastic container and freeze until partially frozen, 2–3 hours. Remove and stir the frozen crystals into the liquid using a fork, then return to the freezer. Continue freezing, stirring the granita two more times during the process, to obtain a granular texture.

NOW PREPARE THE BROWNIE BASE for the parfait. Line eight 1⁵/₈- by 3-inch (4- by 8-cm) rectangular moulds with plastic wrap. Cut out a thin slice of brownie to line the bottom of each one: First cut the brownie into 1⁵/₈- by 3-inch (4- by 8-cm) rectangles; turn one on its side and cut into 3 or 4 thin slices. Repeat to obtain 8 thin slices (you will have some brownies leftover to enjoy the next day!). Press a brownie slice into each lined mould. If you do not have suitable rectangular moulds, line a 4-cup (1-L) loaf pan with plastic wrap, then cut thin slices of chocolate brownie to fit the bottom of the pan.

TO MAKE THE APPLE PARFAIT, prepare a pâte à bombe with the egg yolks and sugar: Dissolve the sugar in ¹/₃ cup (75 mL) water in a heavy-based saucepan over low heat, then increase the heat to high and bring the syrup to a boil. Meanwhile, beat the egg yolks in an electric mixer until pale and creamy. Boil the syrup until it registers 250°F (120°C) on a candy thermometer. With the mixer on the highest speed, slowly trickle the hot syrup onto the egg yolks. Keep on beating until the mixture is thick and smooth and has substantially increased in volume. Beat until the bowl no longer feels hot, then set aside to cool to room temperature.

PEEL, CORE, AND CHOP the apples, squeezing a little lemon juice over them to prevent them from discolouring. Put them in a food processor with the apple cider and blend to a fine, smooth purée. Transfer to a pan and bring to a boil. Cook until the purée has reduced by about half. Meanwhile, soak the gelatin in cold water for a few minutes to soften.

PASS THE REDUCED APPLE PURÉE through a fine sieve into a large bowl, pushing down on the pulp in the sieve to extract all the juice. (If the purée has cooled down, reheat to just below a boil in a pan, then tip into a bowl.) Drain the gelatin and squeeze out excess water, then add to the hot apple purée, stirring to dissolve. Let cool, stirring the mixture every once in a while as it cools.

WHEN THE PÂTE À BOMBE and apple purée have both cooled down to room temperature, fold the purée into the pâte à bombe. Whip the cream to soft peaks, then incorporate the rum a little at a time. Fold this into the parfait base mixture. Spoon into the prepared moulds or loaf pan and freeze until firm.

TO MAKE THE HONEYCOMB TUILES, preheat the oven to 375°F (190°C). Put the sugar, glucose, honey, and 3 tbsp (45 mL) water into a heavy-based saucepan and stir over low heat until the sugar has dissolved. Increase the heat and boil until the syrup registers 335°F (170°C) on a candy thermometer and begins to take on a caramel colour. Whisk in the baking soda until smooth (take care as the mixture will erupt and dramatically increase in volume). Tip onto a rimmed baking sheet lined with a silicone baking mat (or a lightly oiled baking sheet). Let cool completely until the honeycomb is hard and brittle.

BREAK THE HONEYCOMB into smaller pieces. Lightly crush one or two pieces and reserve for decoration. Put the rest of the honeycomb in a food processor and blitz to a fine powder.

CUT A RECTANGULAR TEMPLATE (1⅝ by 3 inches/4 by 8 cm) and set it on a large rimmed baking sheet lined with a silicone baking mat. Sift enough honeycomb powder over the cut-out to get a thin layer. Lift off the template and repeat to make 16 rectangles, or more to allow for breakage (you may need to use two baking sheets). Place in the oven to bake until the honeycomb powder has just melted, about 1 minute. Let cool completely, then lift the rectangles off the silicone mat and store in an airtight container until ready to use.

FOR THE CHAMPAGNE FOAM, put the sugar and milk in a pan over low heat and stir to dissolve, then slowly bring to a boil. Meanwhile, soak the gelatin leaf in cold water to cover for a few minutes to soften. Remove the gelatin and squeeze out excess water. As the milk begins to boil, take off the heat and add the gelatin, stirring to dissolve. Let cool completely.

STIR THE CHAMPAGNE into the milk mixture just as it begins to set, then chill until firm but still slightly wobbly to the touch in the centre, 2–3 hours. Whisk the mixture using an electric mixer, to lighten it. In another bowl, whip the cream until it holds peaks, then fold into the Champagne base. Whisk the mixture until it is light, then chill for a couple of hours before serving.

WHEN READY TO SERVE, brush each serving plate with a strip of melted chocolate and sprinkle with toasted coconut, if you like. Unmould the apple parfaits by rubbing a hot cloth around the sides of the rectangular moulds (or loaf pan). Turn out and remove the plastic wrap. Use a metal spatula to lift each parfait onto a serving plate. (If you have used a loaf pan, trim the edges of the parfait to get straight sides, then cut into thick slices.)

DRIZZLE MELTED CHOCOLATE decoratively over the top of the parfait, then top with a layer of apple granita. Sandwich the parfait vertically with two honeycomb tuiles. Put a neat spoonful of Champagne foam on one side of the parfait and sprinkle a little crushed honeycomb on top. Add a scoop of milk ice cream and decorate with a chocolate spiral, if you like. Drizzle a little reduced apple syrup around the plate, if using. Serve immediately.

BASICS

Fish stock

MAKES ABOUT 4 CUPS (1 L)

2 lb (1 kg) white fish bones and trimmings
   (ideally turbot, sole, or haddock)
2 tbsp (30 mL) olive oil
1 small onion, peeled and chopped
1/2 celery stalk, trimmed and sliced
1 small fennel bulb, trimmed and chopped
1 small leek, trimmed and sliced
Sea salt and black pepper
1/3 cup (75 mL) dry white wine

If using the fish heads, cut out the eyes
and gills and remove any traces of blood.
Heat the olive oil in a large pot and add
the onion, celery, fennel, leek, and a little
salt and pepper. Stir the vegetables over
medium heat until they begin to soften,
3–4 minutes; don't let them brown. Add
the fish bones and wine, and bubble
until reduced right down. Pour in
enough cold water to cover and bring to
a boil, then skim off the scum from the
surface. Lower the heat and simmer for
20 minutes. Remove the pan from the
heat and let the stock settle for about
20 minutes as it cools. Ladle the stock
through a cheesecloth-lined sieve into a
bowl. Keep refrigerated and use within
2–3 days, or freeze in smaller quantities
for up to 3 months.

Shellfish stock

MAKES ABOUT 4 CUPS (1 L)

4 tbsp (60 mL) olive oil
1 lb (500 g) lobster, langoustine (scampi),
   or crab shells and heads (or a mixture)
Bones from 2–3 red mullet
1/2 cup (125 mL) roughly chopped shallots
2 garlic cloves, peeled
1 celery stalk, trimmed and chopped
1 carrot, peeled and chopped
1/4 leek, halved
1/4 cup (50 mL) red sweet pepper
   trimmings
1/4 cup (50 mL) fennel trimmings
1 1/2 tbsp (25 mL) tomato paste
Few thyme sprigs and parsley stems
1 bay leaf
3 coriander seeds
3 white peppercorns
1 star anise
1/2 cup (125 mL) dry white wine or
   Noilly Prat
4 cups (1 L) fish stock (see left)
Sea salt and black pepper

Heat half the oil in a large pan. Add the
shells and fish bones and fry, stirring
occasionally and shaking the pan, until
the shells are bright red. Meanwhile, heat
the remaining oil in a large, wide pot.
Add the shallots, garlic, celery, carrot,
leek, and pepper and fennel trimmings.
Cook until softened, 8–10 minutes.
Stir in the tomato paste and cook for
2 minutes longer. Tip in the herbs and
spices and add the wine. Let bubble until
almost totally reduced, then add the fish
stock. Bring to a simmer, skim off any
scum from the surface, and cook gently
for 30 minutes. Season lightly. Remove
from the heat and let the stock settle for
about 20 minutes as it cools. Pass the
stock through a cheesecloth-lined sieve.
Use as required within 2–3 days, or freeze
in batches for up to 3 months.

Chicken stock

MAKES ABOUT 6 CUPS (1.5 L)

2 tbsp (30 mL) olive oil
1 carrot, peeled and chopped
1 onion, peeled and chopped
2 celery stalks, trimmed and chopped
1 leek, trimmed and sliced
3 garlic cloves, peeled
2 bay leaves
Few thyme sprigs
2 tbsp (30 mL) tomato paste
2 tbsp (30 mL) all-purpose flour
2 lb (1 kg) raw chicken bones (roasted
   if making brown chicken stock)
Sea salt and black pepper

Heat the olive oil in a large pot. Add the
vegetables, garlic, bay leaves, and thyme,
and cook over medium heat, stirring
occasionally, until the vegetables are
golden. Stir in the tomato paste and
flour, and cook for 1 minute longer. Add
the chicken bones and pour in enough
cold water to cover them. Season lightly.
Bring to a boil and skim off any scum
that rises to the surface. Reduce the heat
to a simmer and cook gently for 1 hour.
Let the stock settle and cool down for
20 minutes before passing it through a
fine sieve. Chill and use within 4–5 days,
or freeze in batches for up to 3 months.

Veal stock

MAKES ABOUT 6–8 CUPS (1.5–2 L)
3 lb (1.5 kg) veal bones
7 tbsp (105 mL) olive oil
1 large onion, peeled and roughly chopped
2 large carrots, peeled and chopped
1 celery stalk, trimmed and chopped
4–5 garlic cloves (unpeeled)
1 tbsp (15 mL) tomato paste
3/4 cup (175 mL) Madeira
3/4 cup (175 mL) ruby port
Scant 4 oz (100 g) cremino mushrooms, cleaned
Bouquet garni (bay leaf, thyme, and flat-leaf parsley sprigs)
Sea salt and black pepper

Preheat the oven to 425°F (220°C). Put the veal bones into a roasting pan, drizzle half of the olive oil over them, and roast, turning occasionally, until browned, 1–1½ hours. Meanwhile, heat the rest of the olive oil in a large pot and fry the chopped vegetables and garlic cloves over high heat until lightly coloured. Stir in the tomato paste. Fry the vegetables until golden brown, about 2 minutes longer. Deglaze the pan with the Madeira and port, and boil vigorously until reduced to a syrupy consistency. Drain the roasted bones of excess oil and add to the pot. Pour in enough water to cover (about 20 cups/5 L) and bring to a boil. Skim off the scum that rises to the surface, then reduce the heat to a gentle simmer. Add the mushrooms and bouquet garni. Simmer, skimming every once in a while, until the stock is clear, about 6 hours. Let the stock settle and cool a little, then strain through a cheesecloth-lined colander set over a large bowl. For a more intense flavour, pour the stock into a clean pan and boil until reduced by half. Season lightly. Chill and use within 4–5 days, or freeze in batches for up to 3 months.

Vegetable stock

MAKES ABOUT 6 CUPS (1.5 L)
3 onions, peeled and roughly chopped
1 leek, trimmed and chopped
2 celery stalks, trimmed and chopped
6 carrots, peeled and chopped
1/2 head of garlic, split horizontally
1 bay leaf
1/2 tsp (2 mL) white peppercorns
1/2 tsp (2 mL) black peppercorns
Handful of herb sprigs (such as thyme, basil, tarragon, coriander, and parsley)
Scant 1 cup (200 mL) dry white wine
Sea salt and black pepper

Put all the vegetables in a large pot with the garlic, bay leaf, and peppercorns. Pour in enough cold water to cover (about 8 cups/2 L) and bring to a boil. Lower the heat and simmer gently for 20 minutes. Remove the pot from the heat, and add the herb sprigs, wine, and a little seasoning. Give the stock a stir, then let cool completely. If you have time, chill the stock overnight before straining. Otherwise, pass through a fine sieve once cooled. Use within 5 days, or freeze in batches for up to 3 months.

Lamb jus

MAKES ABOUT 4 1/2 CUPS (1.2 L)
2 lb (1 kg) lamb rib or neck bones
4 tbsp (60 mL) olive oil
1 onion, peeled and chopped
2 carrots, peeled and chopped
1 celery stalk, trimmed and chopped
1/2 head of garlic, split horizontally
1½ tsp (7 mL) tomato paste
1 bay leaf
Few thyme sprigs
Few flat-leaf parsley sprigs
2 cups (500 mL) dry white wine
4 cups (1 L) veal stock (see left)
4 cups (1 L) chicken stock (see left)

Preheat the oven to 400°F (200°C). Put the lamb bones in a large roasting pan and drizzle half the olive oil over them. Roast, turning occasionally, until well browned, about 1 hour. Heat the remaining oil in a large pot, add the vegetables and garlic, and brown over high heat, stirring frequently. Add the tomato paste and herbs, and stir for 1–2 minutes. Deglaze the pan with the wine, then boil until reduced by half. Drain the browned lamb bones of excess oil, then add to the pot. Pour in the veal and chicken stocks. Add a little water, if necessary, to insure that the bones are covered. Bring to a boil and skim off the scum from the surface. Reduce the heat to a simmer and cook until the liquid has reduced by about half, about 4 hours. Let settle and cool slightly, then strain the stock through a cheesecloth-lined sieve. Use within 5 days, or freeze in batches for up to 3 months.

Red wine sauce

MAKES SCANT 2 CUPS (450 ML)

2 tbsp (30 mL) olive oil
3 large shallots, peeled and finely chopped
4 oz (125 g) meat trimmings
  (beef, veal, venison, or poultry)
1/2 tsp (2 mL) black peppercorns
Few thyme sprigs
1 bay leaf
1 tbsp (15 mL) sherry vinegar
  (or red wine vinegar)
3 cups (750 mL) red wine
1 3/4 cups (425 mL) chicken stock
  (see page 246)
1 3/4 cups (425 mL) veal stock
  (see page 247)
Sea salt and black pepper

Heat the olive oil in a wide, heavy-based pan and sauté the shallots until soft and starting to caramelize, 4–6 minutes. Add the meat trimmings and fry for a few minutes until well browned. Add the peppercorns, thyme, bay leaf, and sherry vinegar. Deglaze the pan with the red wine and bring to a boil. Boil the liquid rapidly until reduced by three-quarters to a rich syrupy glaze. Add the chicken and veal stocks and return to a boil. Once again, boil vigorously until the sauce has reduced by half, or until it has reached the desired consistency. Strain through a fine sieve into a bowl and adjust the seasoning. Reheat to serve.

Madeira sauce

MAKES ABOUT 2 CUPS (500 ML)

2 tbsp (30 mL) olive oil
2 large shallots, peeled and chopped
1 bay leaf and few thyme sprigs
1 garlic clove, peeled
4 oz (125 g) meat trimmings
  (pork, beef, or poultry)
1 cup (250 mL) Madeira
2/3 cup (150 mL) port
2 cups (500 mL) veal stock (see page 247)
2 cups (500 mL) chicken stock
  (see page 246)
Sea salt and black pepper

Heat the olive oil in a wide saucepan, add the shallots with the herbs and garlic, and sweat until softened, 4–6 minutes. Add the meat trimmings and fry for a few minutes until browned. Deglaze the pan with the Madeira and port, and let bubble until reduced by two-thirds. Pour in the stocks and bring back to a boil. Reduce by two-thirds or until the sauce has thickened to a syrupy consistency. Pass through a fine sieve into a bowl. Taste and adjust the seasoning.

Truffle-infused Madeira sauce: Add 1–2 tbsp (15–30 mL) truffle trimmings with the stocks.

Herb crisps

Basil, flat-leaf parsley, coriander, or mint
Drizzle of olive oil

Stretch a sheet of plastic wrap tightly over a deep plate. Rub the herb leaves with a little olive oil, then press flat onto the wrap. Microwave until crisp, 2 1/2–3 minutes. Store in an airtight container and use within 1–2 days.

Lemongrass and chervil velouté

MAKES ABOUT 2 CUPS (500 ML)

1 shallot, peeled and sliced
1/2 tsp (2 mL) white peppercorns
1/2 tsp (2 mL) coriander seeds
1 garlic clove
1 bay leaf
Few thyme sprigs
2 lemongrass stalks, split
1/2 cup (125 mL) Noilly Prat
1 cup (250 mL) fish stock (see page 246)
1 cup (250 mL) whipping cream
Sea salt and black pepper
Bunch of chervil, leaves only, chopped

Put the shallot, peppercorns, coriander seeds, garlic, bay leaf, thyme, lemongrass, and vermouth in a wide saucepan and bring to a boil. Let bubble until the liquid has reduced down to a syrupy glaze. Add the stock and boil to reduce by half. Add the cream and simmer until the sauce has reduced to a coating consistency. Taste and adjust the seasoning. Strain the sauce through a fine sieve into a bowl. Just before serving, reheat and stir in the chopped chervil.

Tomato concassé

MAKES ABOUT 5 OZ (150 G)

8 oz (250 g) ripe plum or roma tomatoes

Lightly score a cross on the top and base of each tomato. Put them in a heatproof bowl and pour on boiling water to cover. Leave until the skins can be peeled off easily, 45–60 seconds (no longer or the tomatoes will turn soft). Remove and peel away the skins, then quarter and remove the seeds. Chop into a fine dice. Cover and chill until required.

Tomato sauce

MAKES ABOUT 3/4 CUP (175 ML)
8 oz (250 g) ripe plum or roma tomatoes
1/3 cup (75 mL) olive oil
1 large shallot, peeled and diced
1 garlic clove, peeled and crushed
Sea salt and black pepper

Immerse the plum tomatoes in a bowl of boiling water for 45–60 seconds. Remove and peel away the skins, then quarter them, remove the seeds, and chop the flesh. Heat the olive oil in a pan and gently sweat the shallot and garlic until softened but not browned, 4–6 minutes. Add the chopped tomatoes and season well. Increase the heat and cook until the tomatoes are very soft, 8–10 minutes. Blitz in a blender until smooth, then return the sauce to the pan and heat through. Taste and adjust the seasoning.

Classic vinaigrette

MAKES ABOUT 1 CUP (250 ML)
7 tbsp (105 mL) extra-virgin olive oil
7 tbsp (105 mL) peanut oil
3 tbsp (45 mL) white wine vinegar
Scant 1 tsp (5 mL) Dijon mustard
Sea salt and black pepper

Blend all the ingredients together in a bowl using an immersion blender until emulsified. Pour into a squeezy bottle (or a jar) and keep in the fridge. Shake well before each use.

Port vinaigrette: Boil 2 1/2 cups (625 mL) port in a wide pan to reduce by half, until thick and syrupy. Cool slightly, then blitz in a blender with 7 tbsp (105 mL) classic vinaigrette to emulsify. Pour into a clean squeezy bottle ready for drizzling. Refrigerate, and shake well before each use. Makes about 1 3/4 cups (425 mL).

Pesto

MAKES ABOUT 1 CUP (250 ML)
Heaped 1/3 cup (heaped 75 mL) pine nuts, toasted
1 1/3 cups (325 mL) basil leaves
3 garlic cloves, peeled and chopped
Scant 2 oz (50 g) parmesan, freshly grated
1/2 cup (125 mL) olive oil, plus extra for sealing
Sea salt and black pepper

Blitz the pine nuts, basil, garlic, and parmesan in a food processor to a rough paste, stopping to scrape down the sides a few times. With the motor running, slowly trickle in the olive oil. Season to taste with salt and pepper. If not using immediately, transfer to a clean jar and pour a thin layer of olive oil over the surface; this helps to keep the pesto fresh. Cover, refrigerate, and use within 5 days.

Mayonnaise

MAKES ABOUT 2 1/2 CUPS (625 ML)
4 extra large egg yolks
2 tsp (10 mL) white wine vinegar
2 tsp (10 mL) English mustard
1 tsp (5 mL) fine sea salt
Freshly ground black pepper
2 1/2 cups (625 mL) peanut oil (or light olive oil)

Put the egg yolks, wine vinegar, mustard, salt, and some pepper into a food processor and blitz until the mixture is very thick and creamy. With the motor running, slowly trickle in the oil in a fine, steady stream, followed by 1–2 tbsp (15–30 mL) cold water—this will help to stabilize the emulsion. Taste and adjust the seasoning. Keep refrigerated and use within 3 days.

Basil vinaigrette

MAKES ABOUT 1/3 CUP (75 ML)
1 large bunch of basil, about 2 1/2 oz (80 g)
4 tbsp (60 mL) olive oil
Pinch of fine sea salt
2–3 tsp (10–15 mL) lemon juice, to taste

Strip the basil leaves from their stems, add to a pot of boiling water, and blanch for 40 seconds. Drain and refresh in a bowl of ice water. Drain well and gently squeeze out excess water. Put the leaves into a small food processor with the olive oil and salt, and blend to a fine purée. Press through a sieve into a bowl; discard the pulp. If not using immediately, keep in a jar in the fridge and use within 2–3 days. Add a little lemon juice and shake to mix just before serving.

Tapenade

MAKES ABOUT 9 OZ (275 G)
2-oz (50-g) can anchovy fillets, drained
1 1/3 cups (325 mL) pitted black olives
2 tbsp (30 mL) rinsed and drained capers
1 large garlic clove, peeled and crushed
1 tbsp (15 mL) extra-virgin olive oil, plus extra for sealing

Blitz the ingredients in a food processor until smooth. Store in a jar or squeezy bottle, topped with a drizzle of olive oil. Refrigerate and use within a week.

Shallot confit

MAKES ABOUT 4 OZ (125 G)

5 large shallots, peeled and finely
  chopped
2/3–1 cup (150–250 mL) olive oil
Sea salt and black pepper

In a heavy-based pan, sweat the shallots with 2–3 tbsp (30–45 mL) olive oil until beginning to soften, but not brown. Season well and add enough olive oil to cover. Cook over very low heat until the shallots are translucent and very soft, about 30 minutes. Drain off excess oil before using.

Garlic purée

MAKES ABOUT 6 OZ (175 G)

5 heads of garlic, cloves separated
  and peeled
2 tbsp (30 mL) butter
1 tbsp (15 mL) olive oil, plus extra
  for sealing
7 tbsp (105 mL) vegetable stock (see
  page 247) or water

Gently sauté the garlic cloves with the butter and olive oil in a small pan until lightly golden, 1–2 minutes. Add the stock and lay a crumpled sheet of parchment paper on top. Simmer gently until the garlic is very soft, 10–15 minutes. While still hot, transfer the garlic and half of the cooking liquid and fat to a food processor and purée until smooth. If the paste is too thick, add a little more fat and blitz until you have achieved the required consistency. Cool, then store in a clean squeezy bottle or jar, with a thin layer of oil on top to prevent it from turning brown. Keep refrigerated.

Celeriac purée

MAKES ABOUT 1 1/4 LB (625 G)

1 large celeriac (about 1 lb/500 g)
4 tsp (20 mL) butter
Sea salt and black pepper
1/2 cup (125 mL) whipping cream

Peel and chop the celeriac. Melt the butter in a pan and add the celeriac with some seasoning. Stir over high heat until the celeriac starts to soften, 3–4 minutes. Reduce the heat, add the cream, and cover the pan. Cook until the celeriac is very soft, 15–20 minutes. While still hot, transfer to a food processor and blend to a fine purée. For a smoother result, pass the purée through a fine sieve. Check the seasoning and reheat before serving.

Turnip purée

MAKES ABOUT 7 OZ (200 G)

1 large or 2 medium turnips (about
  14 oz/400 g)
4 tsp (20 mL) butter
Sea salt and black pepper
1/2 cup (125 mL) whipping cream

Peel the turnips and chop into 1/2-inch (1-cm) dice. Melt the butter in a pan and add the turnips with some seasoning. Stir over high heat until lightly golden, 4–5 minutes. Lower the heat, add the cream, and cover the pan. Cook gently, stirring occasionally, until the turnips are very soft, 15–20 minutes. Transfer to a food processor and blitz to a smooth purée. For a very smooth purée, pass through a fine sieve. Check the seasoning and reheat before serving.

Saffron pasta dough

MAKES ABOUT 1 3/4 LB (900 G)

Large pinch of saffron strands
1 lb (500 g) Italian "00" pasta flour
  (about 4 cups/1 L)
1/2 tsp (2 mL) fine sea salt
4 extra large eggs
6 egg yolks
2 tbsp (30 mL) olive oil

Soak the saffron in 1 tbsp (15 mL) boiling water for 5 minutes. Sift the flour and salt into a food processor. Add the eggs, yolks, and oil. Strain in the saffron water. Blitz to combine, stopping twice to scrape down the sides of the machine. The mixture should form small lumps, which will hold together as a smooth, firm paste when pressed. Tip onto a lightly floured surface and knead for a few minutes until smooth and slightly springy. Wrap in plastic wrap and let rest for at least 30 minutes before using.

Tomato chutney

MAKES SCANT 1 CUP (200 ML)

10 oz (300 g) ripe plum or roma tomatoes
2 tbsp (30 mL) extra-virgin olive oil
Few thyme sprigs
Sea salt and black pepper

Put the tomatoes in a heatproof bowl, pour over boiling water to cover, and leave for 45–60 seconds to loosen the skins. Peel off the skins, then quarter, remove the seeds, and finely chop the flesh. Heat the olive oil in a saucepan and add the tomatoes, thyme, and seasoning. Cook until the tomatoes are soft and pulpy, but fairly dry, 5–7 minutes. Remove the thyme before serving.

Tempura batter

MAKES ABOUT 1 3/4 CUPS (425 ML)
Scant 1 cup (250 mL) all-purpose flour
1/4 cup (50 mL) cornstarch
1/2 tsp (2 mL) fine sea salt
Freshly ground black pepper
2/3 cup (150 mL) chilled sparkling water
2/3 cup (150 mL) chilled beer or light ale

Sift the flour and cornstarch into a large bowl and add the salt and pepper. Using a balloon whisk, quickly whisk in the water and ale. To ensure a light result, do not over-mix; the batter should still be slightly lumpy. Use immediately for coating ingredients before deep-frying.

Crème anglaise

MAKES ABOUT 2 1/2 CUPS (625 ML)
1 cup (250 mL) whole milk
1 cup (250 mL) whipping cream
6 tbsp (90 mL) granulated sugar
1 vanilla bean, split lengthwise
6 extra large egg yolks

Pour the milk and cream into a heavy-based saucepan and add 1 tbsp (15 mL) sugar. Scrape in the seeds from the vanilla bean and add the pod, too. Slowly bring to a boil. Meanwhile, beat the egg yolks and remaining sugar together in a large bowl. As it is about to boil, very slowly pour the creamy milk onto the egg mix, whisking as you do so. Strain through a sieve into a clean pan. Stir the custard over low heat with a wooden spoon until it has thickened enough to lightly coat the back of the spoon; do not overheat or it will curdle. Strain through a fine sieve into a bowl and let cool, stirring from time to time to prevent a skin from forming.

Vanilla ice cream

MAKES ABOUT 5 CUPS (1.2 L)
2 cups (500 mL) whole milk
2 cups (500 mL) whipping cream
1 cup (250 mL) granulated sugar
2 vanilla beans, split lengthwise
  (or 2 tsp/10 mL vanilla extract)
12 extra large egg yolks

Pour the milk and cream into a heavy-based saucepan and add 2 tbsp (30 mL) sugar. Scrape the seeds from the vanilla bean and add these to the pan with the pod. Slowly bring to a boil. Meanwhile, beat the egg yolks and remaining sugar together in a large bowl. As soon as the creamy milk creeps up the sides of the pan, remove from the heat and gradually pour onto the egg yolk mix, whisking continuously. Strain the liquid back into the pan. Stir over low heat with a wooden spoon until the custard thickens enough to lightly coat the back of the spoon. Strain the custard through a fine sieve into a bowl set over another bowl of ice water. Stir the custard occasionally as it cools. Pour the cold custard into an ice-cream machine and churn until almost firm. Transfer to a shallow container and freeze until firm. Let the ice cream soften at room temperature for 5–10 minutes before serving.

Stock syrup

MAKES ABOUT 2 CUPS (500 ML)
1 1/4 cups (300 mL) granulated sugar

Put the sugar in a heavy-based saucepan with 2 cups (500 mL) water and dissolve over low heat. Bring the syrup to a boil and boil for 5 minutes. Let cool, then pour into a clean bottle and keep in the fridge for up to 2 weeks. For a reduced stock syrup, boil until reduced by half before cooling.

Dried pear slices

2 cups (500 mL) granulated sugar
Juice of 1/2 lemon
3–4 pears

Preheat the oven to its lowest setting and line 2 baking sheets with silicone baking mats. Put the sugar, lemon juice, and 1 3/4 cups (425 mL) water into a pan and stir over low heat to dissolve the sugar. Increase the heat and boil for 5 minutes until the syrup is slightly thickened. Leaving the skin on, thinly slice the pears lengthwise, using a mandoline or sharp knife. (At the restaurant, we use a meat slicer.) As you cut each slice, immediately dip into the syrup, then lay on the baking sheet. (We also slice through the centre of each pear to get a pretty slice with the core and stem in place.) The syrup can be chilled for up to a week and re-used. Place the pears slices in the low oven to dry until they are firm and can be lifted off the silicone easily, about 2 hours. If they start to turn brown, prop the oven door open to lower the temperature. When cool, store the pear slices in an airtight container, separated by sheets of parchment paper.

GLOSSARY

ACETATE Thin plastic sheets used to mould desserts in the professional kitchen. Tempered couverture chocolate (see below) is generally spread and cooled on acetate sheets to create different shapes or moulds.

BASTE To spoon or brush pan juices or a marinade over food during cooking to keep it moist and succulent.

BIND To mix liquid or a wet paste into a dry mixture, to bring all the ingredients together.

BLANCH To briefly immerse food in boiling water or hot oil to partially cook it so that the outside is soft while the centre is still crunchy. Often the food is immediately refreshed or plunged into cold water to stop the cooking process and retain colour and texture.

CARAMELIZE To cook foods over high heat until the natural sugars have browned. Also, to heat sugar until it dissolves and cooks to a caramel.

CLARIFY To remove solid deposits from food, resulting in a clear liquid. Butter is clarified by melting it and then pouring off the golden oils, often through a cheesecloth-lined sieve. Stock can be clarified by bringing it to a boil with an egg-white mixture, which binds together with the solids, then straining it through a cheesecloth-lined sieve.

CONFIT To cook food slowly, completely submerged in oil or fat, such as melted goose or duck fat, over low heat. Usually, the food is also stored in the same fat or oil.

COULIS A dessert sauce made from pureed fruit, such as berries or mangoes, mixed with some stock syrup.

COUVERTURE CHOCOLATE A good-quality chocolate containing a minimum of 32% cocoa solids. Mostly used by professional pastry chefs or chocolatiers to coat or mould desserts, it has an excellent flavour and a shiny appearance and thin consistency when melted. Couverture chocolate needs to be tempered (see right) in order to achieve a glossy finish and a hard, crisp texture.

DARIOLE MOULD A small metal mould, about 3 inches (8 cm) high, usually with curved sides. The bottom is narrower than the top. Generally used to make individual servings of desserts or savoury mousses.

DEGLAZE To pour liquid, wine, or spirit into a hot pan after it has been used to fry food over high heat. When stirred, the liquid dislodges any sediment stuck on the bottom of the pan. The alcohol is boiled to evaporate, leaving a concentrated flavour in the pan, which enhances the taste of the sauce.

DIGITAL PROBE THERMOMETER A hand-held battery-operated thermometer with a probe attachment, which is used to accurately and instantaneously assess the temperature of solid or liquid food, such as roasts of meat or melted chocolate.

FOLD IN To carefully combine a wet or dry ingredient, or a mixture, into a wet mixture by scooping and turning the combined mixtures with a spatula or a large metal spoon in a figure-of-eight motion.

GIANDUJA (OR GIANDUIA) PASTE A thick paste made from chocolate and hazelnut that is often used to make chilled desserts like ice creams and parfaits, as well as chocolate truffles and cakes. Mostly available in commercial quantities from professional or restaurant suppliers.

INFUSE To soak or steep strong flavourings, such as herbs, spices, or tea, in hot liquid so that they impart their aromas.

JUS The original French term au jus literally means to cook food with its own natural juices. In the culinary world, jus is often used to describe a light meat sauce cooked with additional flavouring, such as vegetables, herbs, wine, and stock.

LARDING NEEDLE A long needle with a hook or clasp at one end. It is used to secure a long strip of food, such as smoked salmon or bacon, which is then threaded through a thick piece of fish or meat.

LIQUID GLUCOSE A viscous syrup used as a sweetener, which also prevents coarse ice crystals in desserts. Glucose helps to achieve ice creams and sorbets with a smooth, velvety finish. Light corn syrup is a type of liquid glucose made from cornstarch.

MACERATE To soak food in liquid or alcohol so it softens and absorbs the flavour of the liquid. Fruit is often soaked in wine, liqueur, or stock syrup to tenderize and provide another flavour dimension.

MILLEFEUILLE French term literally meaning "a thousand layers." Now widely used to describe dishes with lots of layers.

PINK SALT A preserving salt, also known as sel rose, used to retain the vibrant colour of food such as cured meats and foie gras.

POACH To cook food gently by immersing in a liquid such as stock or sugar syrup.

PURÉE To blend or liquefy foods into a smooth paste.

QUENELLE Food shaped into a neat oval using one or two deeply curved spoons to create an attractive presentation.

REDUCE To boil a liquid vigorously until it has evaporated and decreased in volume.

REDUCED STOCK To boil stock until well reduced in volume, leaving a concentrated flavour and a thickened, syrupy consistency. Reduced stock is often used as a glaze for meat dishes.

REFRESH To plunge food into cold water after blanching, to stop the cooking process and preserve the colour and texture.

SCALD To bring a liquid such as milk or cream up to boiling point, just until bubbles begin to appear around the sides of the pan.

SHRED To tear food into small pieces, using two forks moving in opposite directions.

SWEAT To gently fry food with a little oil in a covered pan. The steam in the pan helps to keep the food moist and prevents the food from browning.

TEMPER To take couverture chocolate (see left) through a number of different melting and setting points, which results in changes in the alignment of the molecules in the chocolate during cooling. Once it has set, tempered chocolate has a shiny appearance, breaks with a hard snap, and has a smooth "mouthfeel."

INDEX

ACKNOWLEDGMENTS

Any restaurant, three-star or not, relies on exceptional people—from the kitchen porter to the sous chef to the wait staff at the front of house. I am very fortunate to be surrounded by such people, many of whom have stuck with me through thick and thin since our early days at the Aubergine.

Take for example, Simone Zanoni, who started 12 years ago as my kitchen porter. Simone's infectious energy, tenacity, flair, and creativity have quickly taken him through the ranks of the kitchen hierarchy. He trained hard and it makes me proud to see him running the kitchen now.

Our kitchen at Royal Hospital Road runs like a well-oiled machine, thanks to my Executive Head Chef, Mark Askew, who has also been working with me since the very beginning. I consider Mark to be one of the most consistent and talented chefs in Britain today.

Providing support to both Mark and Simone is Clare Smyth, an inspiring chef whose technical skills are amazing. She has an articulate palate and a calm and composed manner, which sets her apart from other chefs, particularly in a testosterone-driven, male-dominated industry. Following in Clare's footsteps is Angie Steele, our South African chef who has impressed us with her talent and durability. She will lead the team in our Amsterdam restaurant, due to open soon.

Two other chefs I would like to mention are Sean Burbidge and Paul Walsh, both of whom are extremely focused, disciplined, and ambitious. Also thanks to Josh Emett who heads up our restaurant in New York, and Nicolas Defremont who takes care of the dining room there.

If you've ever met the man, you would remember Jean-Claude Breton. One thing for sure, he remembers you. As our top *maître d'*, not only is Jean-Claude incredibly professional, he makes it his mission to remember every guest's name as well as what they had for dinner. Who needs a computer when you've got a memory like Jean-Claude's? As far as I'm concerned, the man could run MI5.

Our three stars would merely be an aspiration if it were not for the phenomenal support we get from our operations and reservations teams. Without the likes of Gillian Thomson and Nicola Monks, we would not be able to focus our attention on cooking and serving fantastic food.

Special thanks to everyone involved in the production of this book: Tony Turnbull my editor at *The Times* who has acquired so much food knowledge he could open a restaurant of his own; Mark Sargeant (or "Sarge" as he is affectionately called), my right hand man who understands me so well; Emily Quah, the "yummy mummy" of the year, whose reliability, dedication, and aptitude is admirable; Janet Illsley for her remarkable efficiency, commitment, and attention to detail; Helen Lewis and Quentin Bacon for making the book look absolutely gorgeous; and to Anne Furniss and Alison Cathie for their support and confidence in this personal endeavor.

Eternal thanks to Chris Hutcheson who makes everything possible, and my extended gratitude to Jo Barnes who patiently manages my PR. And last but not least, thanks to Tana, Megan, Jack, Holly, and Matilda for always being there for me.

Notes

• The recipes in this book, as photographed, originate from Gordon Ramsay, Royal Hospital Road in London. They have been adapted and carefully tested for the domestic kitchen. Nevertheless many of the recipes are still challenging and demand skill and precision on the part of the home cook.

• It is absolutely essential to use good-quality ingredients in prime condition.

• All spoon measures are level unless otherwise stated

• All herbs are fresh, and all pepper is freshly ground black pepper unless otherwise suggested.

• It is recommended that free-range eggs are used. Anyone who is pregnant or in a vulnerable health group should avoid those recipes that contain raw egg whites or lightly cooked eggs.

• Leaf gelatin is available from selected gourmet and cake decorating stores, or it may be sourced online. 4 sheets of leaf gelatin are equivalent to a standard ¼-ounce packet of powdered gelatin.

• Timings are provided as guidelines, with a description of colour or texture where appropriate, but the reader must rely on their own judgment as to when a dish is properly cooked. The oven timings apply to convection ovens. If using a conventional oven, increase the temperature by 25°F (15°C). Use an oven thermometer to check the accuracy of your oven.

EDITORIAL DIRECTOR *Anne Furniss*
CREATIVE DIRECTOR *Helen Lewis*
PROJECT EDITOR *Janet Illsley*
AMERICAN EDITOR *Norma MacMillan*
TEXT: THE 3-STAR EXPERIENCE *Tony Turnbull*
RECIPE RESEARCH AND TESTING *Emily Quah,
   assisted by Cathryn Evans*
PHOTOGRAPHER *Quentin Bacon*
FOOD STYLISTS *Simone Zanoni, Mark Sargeant*
PRODUCTION *Ruth Deary, Vincent Smith*

First published in 2007 by
Quadrille Publishing Limited
Alhambra House, 27–31 Charing Cross Road
London WC2H 0LS
www.quadrille.co.uk

Text © 2007 Gordon Ramsay
Photography © 2007 Quentin Bacon
Design and layout © 2007 Quadrille Publishing Limited

Library and Archives Canada Cataloguing in Publication
Ramsay, Gordon
   Three-star chef / Gordon Ramsay.
Includes index.
ISBN 978-1-55470-090-5

1.Cookery. I. Title.
TX714.R353 2008   641.5   C2008-901734-X

ONTARIO ARTS COUNCIL
CONSEIL DES ARTS DE L'ONTARIO

The publisher gratefully acknowledges the support of the Canada Council for the Arts and the Ontario Arts Council for its publishing program. We acknowledge the support of the Government of Ontario through the Ontario Media Development Corporation's Ontario Book Initiative.

We acknowledge the financial support of the Government of Canada through the Book Publishing Industry Development Program (BPIDP) for our publishing activities.

Key Porter Books Limited
Six Adelaide Street East, Tenth Floor
Toronto, Ontario
Canada M5C 1H6

www.keyporter.com

Printed and bound in China

08 09 10 11 12 5 4 3

OCEAN COUNTY LIBRARY
Jackson, NJ 08527